A VERY SPECIAL GIRL

Deborah stayed the night since her dorm had a curfew hour we'd gone past, and there we were the next morning, alone in the room now, looking at each other in dazed wonder. What was this? More than just a roll in the hay, that was for sure. We had amazed each other.

It was spectacular sex, but there was more. We had been in each other's arms all night, and lazily made love again. She was able to scream a bit this time and that made her happy. I suggested breakfast. She looked at her watch and said, "I have a class." She suddenly seemed unhappy to be there, as if it were all a mistake.

She went into the bathroom and pulled herself together. I got dressed, too. She came out, smiling tentatively and said, "I will date you. But there are conditions."

"Okay. Such as?"

"I am not your girl or your honey or any of that nonsense. There will be no P.D.A. Public displays of affection. You will treat me like a lady and not do guy things to me. No pats on the ass. Not even a kiss on the cheek."

I was bemused. "Okay. I'll try to remember all that."

"If you don't, it's over."

A Perfect Spy

A memoir by

Francis Hamit

BRASS
CANNON
BOOKS

BOOK DESIGN BY LEIGH STROTHER-VIEN

Typeset in Georgia font, a TrueType font.

FIRST EDITION

ISBN 978-1-59595-990-4

Brass Cannon Books
brasscannonbks@earthlink.net

Printed in the United States of America

INTRODUCTION

This is the story of something I did about fifty years ago as a student at the University of Iowa. It is part of my larger memoir, Out of Step: A Memoir of the Vietnam War Years. *I witnessed many of the conflicting and highly charged cultural phenomena of the 1960s. In the course of my personal journey through the events described herein, I experienced heartbreak and made decisions that were undoubtedly unwise since they put me at great risk, personally and professionally. In writing about this, I have relied upon memories that have been compromised not only by the passage of time but by my exposure to Agent Orange and other chemicals during my service in the Vietnam War. I have used documents and news accounts from that era to bolster or retrieve those memories, which are now more re-imagined than recollected. Since I also write fiction those storytelling and narrative techniques may have intruded and altered my rendition of facts, especially where conversations are concerned. Other people who were there may remember some details differently, with equal reliability. The broad outlines of the story are correct. Memories are never entirely accurate. I have spared myself little in terms of personal embarrassment and admitted things that might have been better hidden.*

The Iowa City Police Department says they have no record of my service. This narrative is offered because I thought there should be some kind of record. I leave it to the reader to judge my actions, hoping only that they will be fair and kind. It all happened long ago.

A warning to parents and sensitive readers: there is a lot of sex here. It's also a coming-of-age tale. Names have been changed to protect some friends of that era from having to explain themselves; these are indicated by an asterisk when first introduced.

I am 20 years old when we begin.

CHAPTER 1

Memories are not always golden. Some are tinged with brownish edges as if they had been left in the sun too long. So it is here. As Bob Dylan said, "To live outside the Law, you must be honest." I am often accused of being too much so.

This is the story of how I became a spy. Not a choice I made lightly and not one I regret. It was one of several things that happened to me in Iowa City that changed my life. I loved being there and hoped to make it my permanent home since growing up in the U.S. Army required frequent moves. Life had other plans for me.

I grew up fascinated with intelligence work, but my decision to volunteer myself as a collector of intelligence against the trade in illegal drugs came not so much from the early James Bond and other spy films as it did from the Rudyard Kipling novel *Kim*, about a teenaged boy in 19th Century British India who becomes an operative for the British Secret Service. It seemed like noble work, something worth doing. People mistake this for a child's adventure story because of the age of its protagonist. It is no such thing but rather the first modern spy novel. It engaged me so much that I read it a dozen times or more as a teenager myself to decode its secrets. Kim is motivated by the adventure of "The Great Game" but learns life lessons not just about the trade of spying but about loyalty and honor and friendship. He has no conscious plan for his life at the beginning, but is taken up and set on his path by others, at some risk to his life.

That becoming a "Narc" might be dangerous worried me not at all. I was already oriented toward service in the U.S. military. It was the family business. If you are a soldier of any kind, you accept such risk from the beginning. You play the game for keeps.

I'm the son of a U.S. Army surgeon. As an "Army brat" I grew up at various posts around the USA. Circumstances exposed me to very liberal social influences as a Middle School student at Georgetown Day School in Washington, D.C. and at Tamalpais High School in Mill Valley, California. It was a "liberal" education, one that defied prevailing norms and stereotypes. Tam High was considered the toughest high school in Marin County because we had a significant population of African-American students (simply called "Blacks" or "Negroes" back then). I had Black friends before it was "cool." Some of them were on the stage crew I ran as the stage manager and technical director for the Tam High Drama Department between 1960 and 1963. I was aware of the Civil Rights movement long before it became front page news and was entirely sympathetic with it.

My grades in high school were less than stellar and I hoped to avoid college entirely and simply go to work in Theatre. My father had other plans, seeing my college degree as the fulfillment of his middle-class dream and the proper path toward success. My SAT scores foiled my intention to escape to the world of work and I ended up at the only school that would accept me, a Bible college in the Pacific Northwest where I had a miserable two years before I could escape to the University of Iowa.

Because I was just one of six Drama majors there I was assumed to be a homosexual. I'm not. I was forced to live in a Dorm whose social interactions were modeled on *Lord of the Flies*. I was under 21 years old and under "Loco Parentis" rules because I was legally still a "child." The bullying I experienced there was unremitting. It tested me in a way that no one simply going about his business and trying to get on with his life should ever be tested. It was a small school and I was isolated from any other opportunities for social intercourse. I was not likeable nor could I fend off attacks with humor. I was too angry.

My closest friend there was a gentle, genial young man from Kenya whose true identity was hidden. He'd been a Mau Mau; a terrorist against the British occupation and he was in hiding, concealed and supported by a group of Christian missionaries. He confessed this one night out of loneliness as we were drinking together. I kept the secret since I wasn't sure any of it was true. Regardless, I wasn't going to turn him in. I needed every friend I could get. Kenya became free and he went home, hopefully to a heroes' welcome. I bent my own efforts toward escaping myself and managed it at the end of my Sophomore year. Traumatized but alive.

I arrived in Iowa City in the fall of 1965 tired, out of sorts, and looking to start over. My first two years of college had been successful academically. I was able to transfer out of that small, bigot-laced Bible college where I started my college career and go to Iowa to study stagecraft with A. S. Gillette, the author of my professional bible, *Stage Scenery*. I had major summer job credits, too: I was an Equity apprentice at the famed Alley Theatre in Houston my first summer (1964), and the company stage manager of the Marin County Shakespeare Festival (1965) the second. All well and good, except it had been a horrible two years. The only thing that saved me was that many of the college courses were very good and I'd learned new things about theatre and my other main interest, business. I combined the two by running the college's 900-seat auditorium for a dollar an hour. This did not just continue my career in technical theatre but brought me into contact with several "road and truck" theatrical companies that came there to perform. I could see a future for myself in that profession.

And I did have other work. My father gave me a 35mm camera my senior year of high school and I had to turn pro to afford the film I used. He thought it a more productive hobby than target shooting with pistols and I came to agree. I was a frustrated visual artist, unable to draw what I saw. The camera expanded my creative horizons. But I was too much of an outlier otherwise. I just did not fit in the way I had in high school, where my status was high and I had many friends despite being the ultimate theatre geek.

Iowa City was pleasant and the University of Iowa twenty times larger. It gave me room to breathe and grow.

I was still barely under 21 years old, the age of majority at the time, and once more forced to live in a dorm, with all the pseudo frat-boy nonsense that entailed. I also had to, as part of that package, eat in the cafeteria. Maid service was provided, which meant that I also had no privacy. The contract would last until the following summer. But at least I would be left alone. The University of Iowa campus was very large, diverse, and right next to downtown Iowa City. Escape was a lot easier. I was eager to make new friends and there were dozens of Drama majors rather than six and a dozen faculty members rather than one.

At that time all dorm residents lived under stringent rules from an earlier age, subject to unwanted supervision by student councils who could hand out discipline for minor offenses—a kangaroo court renown for arbitrary decisions. The worst aspect was sexual segregation. No members of the opposite sex were permitted to visit your room, and alcoholic beverages were not permitted. The rooms were Spartan and cold.

I was assigned two roommates. We shared a large room in Quadrangle Hall that was overcrowded, like all the University of Iowa dorms that year, or only two of us would have been assigned to that room. The extra furniture made the room a little too cozy.

We were all new to the University of Iowa. The other two guys were freshmen while I was a junior. Both of them just 18. They were kids compared to me. It was not a good fit.

Wes was a sullen young man from Chicago who didn't have much to say for himself and whom I never got to know well. He didn't last the semester before giving up and going home. I got the impression that college wasn't his idea and had been foisted on him by his parents who wanted to keep him out of the military. The Vietnam War was heating up and he was of draft age. Stories about the war appeared in almost every issue of *The Daily Iowan*, the student newspaper run on big city newspaper principles.

He was a tough kid who really wanted to be a Marine. There was ROTC on campus, but they didn't even want him to join that. The officers trained there would be among the first to be sent into combat. Cyrus Vance, the Deputy Secretary of Defense, said that draftees should also be sent to fight in Vietnam. The fear of being drafted escalated accordingly.

The other kid, Mike, had no worry about being drafted. He was a diabetic, but young and strong. He had to watch his diet and take his shots, but otherwise he had it made. He was blonde-haired and blue-eyed, a big handsome jock with a very happy-go-lucky personality. Nice kid, and his family was very wealthy. His father was the CEO of a big industrial company in New York State. Because of some gifts of stock a decade before, Mike was a multi-millionaire in his own right—but couldn't touch a penny of it. His parents controlled it and used it to keep him on a tight leash. The phrase "helicopter parents" hadn't been invented yet, but they were of that ilk. I had the bad luck to move in at the same time they were getting him settled. (They had flown out on their private jet.)

Apparently he was also a bit of a cut-up because they obviously were concerned about him going astray. Being underage, he had to live in the dorm or a frat. They worried about "the wrong people" and were the worst type of *nouveau riche* snobs. His father was a self-made man, more dedicated to his business and appearances than his son's welfare. He compensated by over-parenting when he could.

Mike's mother was very well-dressed and stern. She demanded to be taken seriously and was hyper-critical and very judgmental. She worried for her son, who was all too eager to cut the apron strings and become a man. To her, he was, and always would be, "her little boy."

Both of them subjected me and Wes to an overreaching third degree. Wes quickly tired of it and excused himself while I was fielding questions about my family, background, and career ambitions. Was Drama a real career? They focused on that rather than my other major, Business. It was good that my father was a doctor but why did he remain in the Army? When I mentioned that he was the new Chief of Surgery at Brooke Army Medical Center in San Antonio, that mollified them somewhat. They understood that better than that he was a Colonel. Like most civilians, they were clueless about military ranks. My own accomplishments meant nothing to them, and Mike's father more or less suggested that I spy on him for them. Money was offered. I declined.

Why would I do that? I wanted him as a friend and ally and already disliked them for their overbearing ways. I decided that it was time to take a stand.

"Look," I said, "Mike seems like a nice kid, but I have a heavy academic load and a heavy rehearsal schedule and I also have to work. I just won't be spending that much time in the room. Get him into a good frat and get them to babysit your kid, if that's what you want, but

I think you should have more faith in him. A lot of kids his age are in the Army. They get treated like adults."

"And why aren't you in the Army?" Mike's mother asked, an edge in her voice.

"My father wants me to be an officer like him. That requires a degree now."

That was not entirely true, but it shut them up and they left, but not before trying to get Mike "more suitable" roommates. Mike told me about this later, laughing. He thanked me for telling them off. For doing what he didn't have the nerve to do, because they controlled his six million dollar fortune until he turned 21 and had big ambitions for him. His life was not his own, but rather planned to the minute going forward for the next 20 years—if they had their way.

But they didn't. They wanted to him to buckle down and study, so his spending allowance was less than mine, and when he found out about my occasional forays into professional photography to make extra money, it gave him insight as to where his true freedom lay. One of the reasons they wanted him to change roommates was that they assumed any male Drama major must be homosexual or a drug addict or both. Mike said he didn't really care, but was visibly relieved when I told him I was neither. That Theatre was, in fact, a great place to meet girls.

I also showed him some of the photography I was doing, artsy stuff mixed with minor-league commercial work. I'd been making money as a freelancer for two years, but was still finding my way, studying the greats and learning how to frame my shots. I carried my camera bag with me most days. He found my slice-of-life, available-light theatre production shots very interesting, but asked why there were so few shots of girls. That also struck him as a way to engage their interest and I agreed. I was hoping to improve my luck that way, too. I did not tell him that at my previous school most of the girls didn't want to spend time with me, much less date me because of the rumors I was Queer, a notion reinforced by the fact that I never seemed to date girls.

I could not tell him what a sexual desert that Bible college had been for me, precisely because I'd been accused, on that same assumption, of being the very thing his parents feared and despised. It was not just whispered but sometimes shouted at me as I walked across campus.

In 1965 being "queer" was still a perversion, a mental illness, and a crime: not just "against nature" but against the law. I had friends who were homosexual, in a very closeted way, in high school. The next town over from Mill Valley is Sausalito so you could usually pick up certain "tells." But friendship trumped prejudice. I was neither disgusted nor attracted to the idea and those guys never bothered with me because they knew I was irredeemably straight. We stayed friends by never talking about the issue. I'd dealt with the issue and the accusations, expressed and implied, by the "mean girls" of all sexes, since getting into theatre at the age of 15, and fended off both advances and heart-broken "what is wrong with me?" confessions along with massive amounts of bullying. That ordeal was considered a rite of passage at the time. *Be a Man*, I was advised. Suck it up and don't let it bother you. I had to leave that bible school to save my sanity. My knuckles were raw from pounding the walls I took my anger out on instead of the bullies who provoked it.

Mike had no problem finding female companionship, but had no money for more than one date a week. Maybe his parents were trying to teach him what it was like to be poor, as they had been at this age. If so, it backfired. He met a girl he really liked and, to get the money to woo her, took a part-time job as a fry cook at the Hamburger Hamlet close to the campus. Restaurant jobs were always available. He liked the work.

By the second semester, he was working full-time and happily flunking all of his courses. He really didn't like school. I liked him, but we were in different worlds and, even as roommates, saw each other infrequently. He may have moved in with his slightly older girlfriend off campus. Hopefully they were happy. I rarely saw him again after that. Toeing the line his parents had so carefully planned did not appeal, and the reality was that, since he was immune to the Draft, he could see freedom ahead. They could hold his money for him until he turned 21, but not take it away. All he had to do to become rich was wait. Hard work did not faze him. Rather, he liked having a job, and he and that girl were in love.

CHAPTER 2

The Drama department at Iowa had changed. Arnie Gillette, my mentor on paper for building sets, was being eased aside; he was close to the mandatory retirement age of 65. I wasn't the only one who wanted to study with him, of course, and most of the others were graduate students in the MFA program. The next chair of the department, Dr. David Thayer, was making changes, and it was no longer as friendly as it had been under Arnie's reign. Most of my classes were in the graying Old Armory building near the Main Library. It also held the Studio Theater and the Film Department. The University Theater was across the Iowa River amongst green trees and lawns. Both were a long hike from the Quadrangle and the cafeteria where I was supposed to take all my meals. Making classes and rehearsals meant skipping lunch or dinner or buying them at the Iowa Memorial Union. That meant finding extra money by working, usually as a freelance photographer.

Another student there was Nicholas Meyer, a playwriting major who already had some one-acts in the Samuel French catalog, and who claimed to have been cheated out of credit for the libretto he wrote at the age of 16 for the musical *Baker Street* (which was, of course, about Sherlock Holmes). No one believed that then, but he would later become world famous as a screenwriter and director and write two best-selling novels about Sherlock Holmes. Ironically, he professed to hate science fiction when I first knew him, but it would be in that genre that he would have his greatest successes. He was brash, arrogant, opinionated, and a bit hard to like, but the same could have been said of me. Perhaps we were too much alike to be friends, or perhaps it was that we were rivals for the affections of a girl we both wanted. She played us against one another but ultimately chose another guy and eventually married him.

Nick also wrote film reviews for *The Daily Iowan* and presented his one-act plays in the Studio Theater. He was much more of a presence than any tech theatre student ever could be. I was simply a tech and had no ambitions to write anything beyond my class assignments. My grammar, punctuation, and spelling were all terrible and I had been repeatedly discouraged from attempting anything creative that involved the English language. Another reason I took to photography so eagerly. It scratched a creative itch within me.

I was also expanding my horizons into acting and directing. I landed a bit part in *The Devil's Disciple,* a Bernard Shaw play, and in *Romeo and Juliet,* which I had been in before and knew by heart. I had directing class projects that were produced for a single afternoon performance in the Studio Theater. My best effort was "Ballad of the Sad Café," by Carson McCullers, marred only by casting the wrong actor to play the malignant dwarf character. He was an undersized 12-year-old boy rather than an adult dwarf and simply could not carry the role. You learn from your mistakes. I took the hit and moved on.

Any proposed project there underwent a trial by fire. Fire from the professors on the selection committee who really challenged you with academic questions as well as technical ones. Most of my classes were in the morning with rehearsals in the afternoons and evenings. That kept me very busy.

CHAPTER 3

The war in Vietnam began to heat up, with fresh news daily. Despite the fact that my father was an army officer, I didn't get involved with, or protest against, the rising tide of sentiment against it. Officers didn't do politics or policy; they served the nation. As his son, anything I said would come back on him, so I simply declined to talk about it. That took some effort on my part because uninformed statements about the U.S. military made me see red sometimes.

The Students for a Democratic Society (SDS) chapter formed at Iowa was part of a national organization that seemed to spring from nowhere. It was soon competing for space on the front page of the student newspaper along with news from the war and the civil rights conflicts in the South. I was sympathetic to that cause because I had Negro friends from high school, but again could not become an activist without endangering my father's military career. And the Young Americans for Freedom, a right-wing group that supported the war, was equally beyond the pale, if I had been so inclined. Being a life-long Democrat from Marin County, California, I was not going that way. I simply did not do politics. I concentrated on my craft.

The Drama department was my entry into the local party scene. Lots of beer and booze, lots of intensive conversation, and lots of opportunities to meet members of the opposite sex. I was out of practice for dating, but after the parties were the late-night gatherings for pie, coffee, and conversation. There you could also find friends. I began to enjoy being with people again since I was no longer a target for scorn and derision. I began to relax and actually enjoy being in a higher education environment.

The party scene back then was very unhealthy. Everyone smoked tobacco and people who preached against it were considered quaint or boring. Everyone drank too much and that led to a lot of sexual fumbling in dark rooms and hallways, sometimes with girls you'd known for all of half an hour. It was Iowa but the rules were changing.

One bad habit I've always had is falling in love too quickly with the wrong girl. I was far more of a romantic than those cold-eyed sorority vixens who measured every man they met for the role of husband and provider. They were after a "MRS" degree.

I got crushes and often got emotionally crushed as well. So it was at The Alley Theatre and again at the Marin County Shakespeare Festival. Was I needy or horny? Probably both. I liked sex. Being young and naive I mistook it for Love.

My hunger for even the sight of female flesh started me going to strip clubs when I was in Houston because I'm a very visual person. It would be one of my principal forms of entertainment for the next two decades. I admired the dancers but the closest I got to dating any of them was when two of them came into the audience to ask if I knew where they could buy marijuana. I didn't, and wouldn't have, so that went nowhere. My beard and long hair misled them, they said. I said, no, I'm an actor, not a hippie. They were very disappointed. So was I for different reasons. I was fascinated by their free-spirited displays and sexual power. I had no more hope of holding them than a butterfly. But I like to look. Especially at beautiful women. Especially when they are taking their clothes off. Watching them has never lost its charm for me.

I also had a hankering to settle down and wanted a regular girlfriend again. I met girls in classes and at parities and just hanging out. Everyone was looking for someone but I was going from a sexual desert to an embarrassment of riches and there were girls who enjoyed breaking hearts and teasing men. I learned caution. My life was chaotic, and stability was an unfulfilled desire. Until I got back to Marin County the summer before, I hadn't had sex in almost two years.

My crushes that were only partially driven by hormones. Aesthetics also played a part, as did drink, which easily overcame judgment on both sides. Sober reflection after a one-night stand leading to a "let's just be friends" parting was the usual result. Sometimes it actually happened that way too. Such friends became confidants. You'd already seen each other naked. What else was there to hide?

The Sexual Revolution started by Hugh Hefner, Kinsey, and Masters & Johnson was under way, and I was eager to enlist. So were many of the girls I met at Iowa, but the terms of engagement had not been set, and this confused everyone. There was an unspoken rule that there had to be at least three dates before you could call yourselves a couple.

That fall I was far too busy to do any serious dating. I had courses in acting, directing, film, photography, and dance, and—on the business side of my education—in management theory. I was overeager to learn everything, so with core courses included, I had 18 semester hours. Lots of study and homework. Lots of rehearsals. Very little sleep and an irregular diet because I was also freelancing as a photographer and doing other odd jobs.

There was a particular bookstore, *The Paper Place,* that I liked because it reminded me of the ones from my high school years in Marin County. It was a gathering place for intellectuals and the arts community. It was owned by a kindly older man, Jerry Stevenson. He carried the kind of novels and poetry books that were in short supply at Hawkeye Books and Iowa Book & Supply, both of which were very University oriented and made most of their revenues by selling textbooks. Jerry Stevenson did not mind if you browsed or just hung out. He liked conversation and was a graduate student himself. He never talked down to others and he would talk with you about anything. He was also a writer and painter and sponsored poetry readings. These, too, were a place to meet people, especially girls, and to get invited to parties. I had a social life again.

What spare time I had left, I spent hanging out at the Iowa Memorial Union. This was another place where various tribes from the Art, Drama, and English Departments gathered and intermingled. You could have a meal or a great conversation or simply lounge at the tables and enjoy the byplay and the passing parade. I was already a close observer: a people watcher.

The memorial was for Iowa graduates who'd died in the service of their country in previous wars. The University was a land-grant college and required to have ROTC and military training. Students who chose ROTC received pay and an early start on an officer's career. It was a four-year program, so one had to start as a freshman. I'd grown a full beard to try and fit in and shaving did not appeal to me. Also, I was too old.

As an undergraduate, my participation in Drama department productions as a technician was usually limited to class-generated projects in the little Studio Theater in the Old Armory building near the library. The real action was across the river at the University Theater. I was, as I had been so many times before, "the new kid" and chaffed at being shut out of jobs I'd known how to do since high school. No one knew me and there was an unconscious bias toward those who had proven themselves in previous productions. I was eventually permitted to help build sets at the big theater. Higher-level crew jobs were reserved for students in lighting, sound, and design classes. Because I had transferred in, I was mistaken for a Freshman until I complained a little. Theoretically I would graduate in 1967. I needed more credits as a theater technician to finally get a real job in New York City or Los Angeles or to go on to graduate school. Or so I thought at the time. The reality was that academic credentials did not count for much in the theatrical "real" world back then. My grades were not good enough to get me into graduate school. Further, no one understood why I was "wasting time" with business courses.

Since I had a deep and comprehensive knowledge of technical theatre and had more than a dozen other stage productions on my résumé, I was excused from the introductory course in stagecraft and simply allowed to go to work on smaller productions. One of them was an experimental play by the poet Donald Justice, who was a professor at the Iowa Writers' Workshop, an institution which—until the moment I met him—I had never heard of.

The rehearsals had to be scheduled around other productions, and Prof. Justice, being from another department, had to take Hobson's choice. He got odd Monday and Tuesday nights and weekend days, but it was a short experimental play with one actor and the hard part was getting the tech right. He asked me to do that for him.

I was glad to help but I had a problem. The resident assistant at my part of the Quadrangle Dorm caught me playing penny-ante poker. This was another "bad" habit I'd acquired at my first school. It was "gambling," and this self-righteous prig put me on restriction for the rest of the semester. I was allowed to go to classes and the cafeteria, but otherwise supposed to be in my room, studying. And he did check to see if you were there.

We had a big argument over whether or not play rehearsals were class-related or a now-forbidden extracurricular activity. I had to appeal over his head to get that permission, but I needed a note for every production. So I asked Don Justice for one, and he was perplexed and then amused. He scribbled one for me, and then said, "You like to play poker, huh?"

"I do," I replied.

"Are you any good?"

"I win more than I lose," I replied, a bit cocky.

He smiled. "There is a regular game for the Poetry Workshop every Thursday night," he said. "You're certainly welcome to come. You helped me, so I will help you."

"I'm still under restriction."

"I'll write you a note. For a special seminar in probability and the redistribution of wealth."

"Sounds like an Econ course."

"Oh, it is. But there is poetry in it, too, as there is in most things. We do experiment a lot with new course concepts at Iowa."

Seeing my hesitation, he added: "Being poor poets, we don't play high stakes. It's a nickel, dime, quarter game. The most you can win or lose in a night is about forty dollars."

That was still a lot of money for me. The minimum wage at the time was $1.25 per hour, and you could pay a week's rent for an off-campus apartment for forty bucks. But he had called my bluff, so I started attending that Thursday night game, which led me to start going to poetry readings to understand what the other players were talking about. They were a form of performance that I wanted to understand.

CHAPTER 4

At that poker game, I met, and quickly came to despise, the then-famous novelist Nelson Algren. His best-selling and most significant work was *The Man with the Golden Arm*, a novel about heroin addiction. I think he's largely forgotten now, like so many of his contemporaries, but an offer to come teach fiction at the Iowa Writers' Workshop had drawn him to Iowa City. He was newly married to a very nice woman who was given an adjunct position in the Drama Department. She taught speech and was prepping the actors in the forthcoming University Theater production of *Romeo and Juliet* about the proper way to pronounce certain Elizabethan words and still be understood in the back row. Very nice lady, but since I had done three other productions of that play, including featured roles, she didn't think I needed her help. I never got to know her well.

Algren was quoted in *The Daily Iowan* that he would probably spend more time discouraging uncreative people than encouraging creative ones. That attitude did not serve him well in a program with a very select group of graduate students who were all certifiably creative and would not have been there otherwise. The Iowa Writers' Workshop is the oldest MFA program in Creative Writing, and is notoriously difficult to get into, even 50 years later. It rejects over 90% of all applicants.

Don Justice had been teaching there for years and was both respected and loved by all.

Algren was a "man's man," a short, thin, pugnacious, swaggering bully who drank too much and gambled too often. He was playing poker at the Elks Lodge as well, and thought our friendly little game too tame. He demanded the stakes be raised and tried to bully Don by making spurious comments about his courage and sexuality. It was a very tense moment. The room was silent as he tried to bully Don, who was shy and quiet, but no coward. He suddenly agreed to the higher stakes. Algren flopped out a wallet loaded with cash. No one was intimidated, but he'd destroyed the friendly little game we liked and made it something dark and hostile.

Everyone was game to take this interloper down. He needed a sharp lesson. Don Justice was a brilliant poker player. Poetry is mathematics and observation for the most part, and under his seemingly timid exterior beat the heart of a warrior.

The Poetry Workshop poker game was normally just for the students and faculty of same. Outsiders such as Algren and me were there by invitation only, and on sufferance. It was another place where I made some real friends in Iowa City, and it was an honest game, unlike the ones at my previous college. It was also friendly, just a bunch of guys who liked to play for small stakes, so no one got hurt. There were several future winners of the Pulitzer Prize and other awards at that table, but—unlike the Drama Department—the competition was limited to how much skill each of us had. Everyone was polite and kind. I liked those guys, and was proud to be in their company. And Nelson Algren was the barbarian at the gate.

We systematically gutted Algren like the fish he was. When Don dropped out with a bad hand, one of the other regular players would step up and take him on. Understand, no one cheated the man. He cheated himself by showing up drunk for the game and then going all-in, often without even looking at his hand. This continued until he ran out of money. It was as if he wanted to lose and be humiliated. We thought the point had been made, but he was there the following week to lose more. His pride wouldn't let him quit. He kept coming back. By the end of the semester, it was said that he had lost his entire teaching salary and half of his wife's, playing bad poker. It was a short marriage.

I think this is where I first realized that great writers are often not great people. There was an entire school of thought at the time that postulated that to be a great writer you had to be a drunk. And maybe a bad-ass as well, willing to engage in manly fisticuffs and other rude behavior. Algren never offered to fight Don Justice or any of the rest of us because he thought us all sissies and real men didn't fight weaklings. He was simply bad-tempered and famous for feuds with other Chicago writers and the Chicago *Sun-Times* before coming to Iowa City. He was also getting old (he was in his mid-50s). So it was just as well that he did not fight: it would not have gone well for him. Several of the regular players would have enjoyed beating the crap out of him on the street outside as well as at the table.

He would later write bitter untruths about the Writers' Workshop. I think his well-deserved humiliation at the Poetry Workshop poker game was behind most of that, although the word was that his teaching also stank.

I came away with enough extra cash from those games to start modestly investing in the stock market. I was 21 now and of legal age to do so. My previous investments had been done through my father, whose idea of a "flyer" was RCA stock at 25—where it had stayed for the previous three years. I wanted a bit more action. I set up an account at a local brokerage to test my skills, and confused everyone by carrying around the *Wall Street Journal* and a copy of Stanislavski's *An Actor Prepares*. I was still trying to master that art and acquire the self-discipline and "all-in" nerve that makes a good actor. I ultimately failed because I didn't like making a fool of myself in front of others. I'd been better and braver in high school, but two years at the bible college had rubbed me raw and made me too sensitive. I did not love doing it the way great actors do and was not willing to settle for being second-rate.

CHAPTER 5

Another visiting professor that year was Gert Weymann of the Berliner Ensemble in East Berlin. He was lean, of medium height with short brown hair and spoke English without any noticeable accent. He blended in well and looked like any other academic.

He brought with him a play by Bertoldt Brecht called *Puntilla and His Hired Man*. This had premiered at that theater several years before, but had not won the acclaim that *Mother Courage and Her Children* and other Brecht plays had. This was the first production in English, but it was deemed too experimental and controversial for the University Theater, so it became a Studio Theater production. It was a Marxist play about class struggle directed by a vetted Communist from behind the Iron Curtain, and this was still Iowa. Weymann compounded the problem by alluding to the ongoing racial difficulties in the U.S.: he made Matti, the hired man, a Negro. That was also a problem. It was allegedly a comedy and with what was going on the American South in April of 1966, no one was laughing. People were being killed out there. There was a collective guilt among Iowa students for not joining the struggle for Civil Rights that the SDS was able to turn to advantage and redirect toward the anti-war movement.

Weymann directed in a style that drove the Method-trained cast a bit nuts. I was cast in a minor role and his constant interruptions and touching me to adjust every motion of my hands and body were so intrusive and counter-productive to the way we had learned to build and sustain a character, that we were reduced to being robots. This was the style he brought with him from Brecht. An actor was not supposed to become his character but stand outside of it. These were two mutually incompatible goals. Despite our frustration no one quit. He was a guest and a professor, and any display of artistic temperament would have been a black mark against us for other productions. And you had to perform to graduate.

Weymann was a charming guy on his own and very patient with these poor Americans. He was careful not to talk about politics and the play was performed a few times and then closed before certain Republican legislators in the Iowa state legislature could get wind of it. Weymann was a visiting professor. *Puntilla* aside, he gave a few lectures and threw a big cast party on the closing night. He was complimentary to all, and thought I was rather old for a student.

I was surprised.

"How old do you think I am?"

"About 32."

"I'm 21."

"You look much older and seem very mature."

"I'm usually the stage manager on a show, not one of the cast."

"Ah," he said, "Then you have gravitas, that authority." He paused a moment, "How old is *Eine Frau*?"

"I don't have a wife."

"The girl you are with? You seem very close."

"Helga? I don't know. A little older. She's a graduate student and I'm a junior. Maybe 25."

Helga* was working on a MFA in Costuming and we'd met working together on *Romeo and Juliet* when I had to be fitted for my costume. In fact, Helga was 32, something I didn't know until after the first time we made love at her trailer in the mobile home park close to the airport. She was moderately pretty with light brown hair, green eyes, and a nice body. She was shy, which was unusual in that department, where most women were actresses who were always "on stage." She was half a foot shorter and obviously found me attractive. That made me pay attention to her. It was also her first year there and she was lonely. She was the first friend I made in the Drama Department. We could talk shop together.

She also assumed that I was her age. She gave me a ride back to the dorm from rehearsal a few times and one night the hug and kiss on the cheek went to the next level and we were making out in the front seat with me feeling her up and her responding in kind. It was very cramped, so she simply adjusted her clothes and drove us back to her place. I was kind to her but also vigorous. She had recently divorced a much older man and had no children. Our affair, which was more sexual than romantic, continued for several weeks into the following semester. She knew less about how her body worked than I did, and was very shy in bed because of a repressive religious upbringing.

I wanted to photograph her for my Creative Photography class but she refused. Posing for nude photographs? The very idea made her blush bright red.

But she wanted to change her nature, feeling that she might be missing something. Sex was everywhere and she wanted her share and then some. Many women did.

We were sort of a couple, but not exclusive to each other. Her idea. She wanted to be "liberated," so I was careful not to fall for her. I certainly didn't mention her to my parents. The age difference would have freaked them out. I simply decided to enjoy the ride.

I also appreciated one more thing about her. She didn't do drugs. She also didn't drink nor smoke. Those were also against her religion.

The sudden rise of the drug culture caught me off guard and dismayed me. Drugs were everywhere. Even Gert Weymann found some for his party and there was a miasma of smoke in the room as the braver souls toked up. He also put something in the punch to loosen inhibitions. With a more sophisticated crowd, it might have become an orgy, but this was Iowa. When I told him that was why things were not going that way, he decided it was time to call it a night, "before they start shitting on the floor."

What the hell kind of parties do they have in East Berlin? I wondered, and what was in that punch, that tasted so nasty that I had just a sip and got a beer instead? He was likeable, but then devils are: it's part of their craft. I later wondered if he might have had another agenda. The University of Iowa was also a major center for research for the Defense Department and other U.S. Government agencies but the students and faculty for the sciences might as well have been on another planet where those in the arts were concerned. We did not know them, or they us.

CHAPTER 6

Helga and I continued on as lovers, more or less in private since she feared criticism from her peers and professors. She had a small blue car and took me home about once a week. Otherwise she was shy of me and blushed pink if I whispered in her ear in public. Other girls in the Costume Design program teased her about our relationship.

During the spring semester I was confronted with the requirement that I take a course in dramatic theory. My bent was more toward the practical than the theoretical, but I had an out: the course in Beginning Playwriting. It was easy, I was told by other students. All you had to do was write a one-act play. No other tests or papers.

The instructor was Dr. Howard Stein. He started the first lecture by writing four words on the blackboard that would change my life.

"What would happen if . . ."

And he gave an example. "What would happen if," he said, "there was this high school kid who was a brilliant sculptor, living in a small town in Iowa, and he created this life-sized work of art, a realistic nude, with his girlfriend's face on it . . . and she's the preacher's daughter? What happens next? What are the complications and how does the story end?"

He went on to explain that this was a premise, where the play began, and that the course would cover the techniques used to turn any premise into a drama or a comedy.

I was hooked right there. I had been in a lot of plays but had never given thought to how they were made. I worked my way through the readings and rather than go home for the ten-day spring break, stayed with Helga at her trailer and wrote a play. It sort of got away from me, and ended up being three acts rather than one. Helga typed it up for me; I could tell from her grimaces that she didn't think it was very good but was too polite to say so. She edited the text and put it in a professional format for me. I was simply hoping for a grade of "C" so I would have the dramatic theory requirement fulfilled.

Stein's reaction to my play was brutal and unexpected. He was not happy with me or the play and said, "Hamit, I will not give you an A on this piece of crap. It's horrible. Your dialog is from hunger or bad television and your characters are cardboard. Three acts is overkill for a plot this thin and you should cut it, but unlike everyone else in the class, you actually had a plot. It has a beginning, a middle, and an end. You understand structure. I know you worked very hard on it, but the best grade I can give you is a B-plus."

I stood there, a little stunned by his outburst, unable to say anything. I'd just been severely criticized for exceeding my own expectations and it was very disorienting.

He shook his head, turning over my bound manuscript in his hands. "Look, kid. I don't know if you have any talent for this or not. I can't tell from this. It's too raw. But there is a fiction writing class this summer. Why don't you stick around, take it, and find out?"

That was a life-changing moment because I did exactly that. By the fall semester I was in the Undergraduate Writers' Workshop. By then I was looking to make a change from Drama, or at least take a break. I was discouraged and burned out. I started writing other things. Experimenting with various kinds of narrative.

And the cause of my discontent with Drama was the result of my own overweening ambition. I persuaded Arnie Gillette to let me run a

University Theater production, *The Inspector General* by Nikolai Gogol. The Studio Theater was smaller than the house I had run at the bible college and I really needed big stage experience on my résumé when I started looking for a regular job. There was a revolving stage at the University Theater that made scene changes easy. You could put two or three sets on it and make the changes mechanically and quickly. The play is a comedy, so split-second timing was also important.

The graduate students in technical theatre were outraged. I was invading their turf, and who the hell was I? They felt that the job should go to one of them and burnish their résumés instead. There was a tradition and a hierarchy to be observed. One of them threatened to check out my résumé, accusing me of exaggerating my credentials. I took that insult very seriously. Another threatened me with physical violence, screaming at me at a rehearsal and inviting me outside to fight. He also called me a "Queer." I declined, of course. Not from any fear of him. I could have taken him easily. But my management courses had taught me that this was not what effective managers did. It would undermine my authority. It made me furious to be challenged that way in front of the rest of my crew. It caused me to say to Arnie Gillette, "Keep that son-of-a-bitch away from me. I won't be responsible if he comes at me again!" And I meant every word of that.

That put Arnie in a terrible position. His authority had also been challenged, but kicking this guy off the crew meant that he failed the Advanced Technical Theatre course and might not get his degree. It might have been smoothed over if the offender had cooled off and shut up. He didn't. He continued to threaten me and stir up bad feelings. And while he was not there when the big revolving stage was operated, his friends made sure that the scene changes were off just enough to make me look bad. I was in charge and gave the cues. I got chewed out in rehearsals and, after the less-than-perfect opening night, replaced.

Arnie knew what had happened. There was a rebellion underway. He was old and tired and didn't have the stomach for it, so he gave in. I had been set up. I began to question my career choice.

This was not the way it was supposed to be. Producing a play is hard enough without such nonsense. It went against everything I'd learned about stagecraft and theatre. We were supposed to support each other, not play games that hurt the production. It was a heartbreaking and humiliating moment for me, the first big failure of my six-year-long career. I was burned out, needing a break and a new girlfriend. Helga dumped me because she could not afford to get crossways with that cabal. She already had my replacement waiting in the wings. I found it very easy to let her go. It was just sex, after all, and not particularly good sex because of her many inhibitions.

CHAPTER 7

I was already involved with another girl, a singer named Elise*.
Her I could have really fallen in love with, because she was beautiful,
young, talented, and knew her power. She loved to flirt . . . and to tease
men. She liked having several guys at her beck and call—a Queen Bee.
I didn't play that game since I had no time. We met when I took some
publicity shots for her and I played it cool with her, pretending
boredom to keep her off balance. And I charged her my regular rates
for the photos; I am a professional, I told her, and professionals get
paid. She was not so much a bitch as a willful child and hanging out
with her had its moments. She sang with the voice of an angel. She was
interesting and intelligent when she wanted to be. I enjoyed talking to
her even after it became obvious that I would never actually manage to
seduce her. We played the game of Flirt.

All of this would not be worth noting here if she hadn't gotten
busted by the Iowa City Police Department for marijuana
possession—at the time, a felony. She was facing as much as five years
in prison. That would destroy her, but she was oblivious. She simply
didn't believe she was in trouble. Perhaps it was the drugs, because she
was suddenly high much of the time from grass provided her by guys
who wanted to get in her pants . . . and did.

The cops offered her an out. Give them the name of her dealer and
it would all go away. She, being deeply and fundamentally stupid in a
way I hadn't seen until then, refused to do so. He was a friend. Friends

didn't betray friends. Her parents couldn't move her on this, and neither could I nor anyone else. She liked the attention and the martyrdom and took no heed of the real consequences, the ruin that would befall her.

Nor was she the only one. Others from the Drama department were caught in the same trap. People I liked. The summer before, at the Marin County Shakespeare Festival, I had experienced some problems with people who were also getting into drugs. Some of the kids I'd been in high school with and been in productions with, not from my class but the ones that immediately followed. The drug culture came on that fast, helped by a shift in popular culture led by Timothy Leary and others who advised them to "tune in, turn on, drop out." LSD was Leary's drug of choice and also pervasive. The constant publicity about drugs created both curiosity and demand for a fresh thrill. The local cops were overwhelmed, trying to stop it. Hence their rather heavy-handed tactics with the students, who were the best market for grass, then LSD, and then cocaine and heroin. It was not an automatic progression generated by taking drugs, but there is a reason that dealers are also known as "pushers." The first hit was always free.

A survey published in *The Daily Iowan* noted that over half of the entire student body that year admitted to having tried marijuana at least once. The cop's focus on the students in theatre might have been provoked by our casual attire, long hair, and beards. We did look like Hippies, who were the new sensation and becoming a popular culture meme.

The Iowa Memorial Union was the daytime place to hang out with your friends and some of mine were very colorful. One was Mark Malcas, a rather flamboyant, openly homosexual poet who seemed to be constantly engaged in pushing the boundaries of acceptable behavior. He was the self-professed poster child for decadence of all kinds; it was simply his way of demanding the attention he'd craved and been denied in childhood. He was there to shock you, but I'd seen more radical performances on the North Side of San Francisco and in Sausalito. I was not impressed, which he took as a challenge.

Mark had the golden skin of his Greek forefathers and carefully groomed coal-black hair and eyes. He wore purple eye shadow and lipstick and was always "on." A natural performance artist. He professed to have a boyfriend, a very handsome ex-Marine who'd allegedly been given a bad-conduct discharge for being Queer, and a girlfriend who also had a girlfriend. Said girlfriend would make out with both of them in public sometimes, looking over her shoulder to see who was watching. Was this performance art or early activism? No one knew and few cared. Mark simply craved attention and got it by pushing boundaries. He was amusing and never vicious. I enjoyed his company. We became friends because we simply liked each other. He was an incorrigible gossip and loved to play the arch Queen commentator on those who passed by. Bitchy, yes. Mean? Never.

On campus, behavior that would get you arrested a few blocks away downtown was not just tolerated but considered daring. "Freedom of expression" also permitted huge license for acting stupid. The Greeks had their houses where they drank and practiced various cruelties on each other in the name of fraternity or sorority. Drinking to excess was part of that culture. An open rebellion against the stricter morals and strait-jacket conventions of the 1950s also contributed to a dramatic shift in behaviors. We had our own local Playboy magazine clone, *The STUDent*, with a topless centerfold of a local sorority girl. "Topless" entertainments were springing up all over the country. It was very sensational since, before then, bare breasts in public were *verboten*. The cultural walls were coming down.

The music, rock and roll, inspired more willingness to experiment and throw off the old restrictions, but it was amplified by the drugs that were suddenly everywhere.

The Pentacrest part of the campus—right next to the Iowa City downtown, where most students who could lived in off-campus apartments and threw parties where anyone was welcome—had a Fellini-like atmosphere at twilight where you would see many interesting things. I recall a slender brunette who wore skin-tight leather jeans and boots and nothing above the waist, walking through the twilight mist, carrying a coiled bullwhip. She never stopped to talk to anyone as she stalked across that huge lawn. Nor did anyone talk to her. She just looked scary. Maybe that was her point. Sex is dangerous.

There were also boys and girls who would meet for the first time walking there and sometimes, without anything said, begin making out. The sexual repression and social conventions of the 1950s were not only being mocked, but destroyed.

Iowa City at the time was considered a refuge for the homosexual community. I learned this from Mark Malcas; it was the one safe stopping place between Greenwich Village in New York City and the Castro in San Francisco. It was the mid-point more than a refuge but there was grudging tolerance—rather than outright hatred and violence—as long as it was not rubbed in the faces of the townspeople. The University was, by far, the biggest employer in town. It set the tone for tolerance. If you stayed downtown, close to the campus, you were safe. This acceptance helped loosen what passed for morals in the straight community as well. Suddenly everything was permitted, if not approved, and limits could be tested. Everything became a grand social experiment.

"Sexual freedom" was the new mantra and concepts such as "open marriage" and polyamory were being openly discussed. No one was revolted. Many were intrigued. Robert A. Heinlein's *Stranger in a*

Strange Land was a best-seller; so were the works of Robert H. Rimmer, especially *The Harrad Experiment,* which was about four students at an elite college whose sex lives were far more interesting than our own. It sold over three million copies. The commune movement was starting up and the "Summer of Love" in San Francisco was just two years away.

The idea of multiple female partners who were not jealous of each other certainly appealed to me, but I was young and had lots of energy and, when it came to sex, no more sense than any other young man my age. My hormones demanded I suspend judgment until they were satisfied, and they almost never were. I did have a few rules. I tried to be kind and a gentleman. I did not date women who were seriously involved with other guys. I tried to avoid women with big problems. Drugs and angry boyfriends were at the head of that list. Jealousy was out of fashion. Boring and uncool. Sex was everywhere and everyone rushed in, afraid to be left out.

Pornography began to emerge from the shadows and be openly read, especially if it was "literary." Henry Miller's *Tropic of Cancer* was used as a text in an advanced English class. "Fanny Hill" [*Memoirs of a Woman of Pleasure*], which had originally been published in the 18th Century, became a best-seller and a landmark Supreme Court case. The elegant and terrifying French novel about sexual submission, *The Story of O,* was widely read and sometimes clumsily imitated. And we were in Iowa!

Sex, drugs, and rock and roll. Folk music, the staple of my high school years, was going away, and the new music more or less demanded drug use. Using drugs made you "cool" and accepted. At least that was the theory. It was a cultural revolution that would soon become political. Unlike almost everyone I knew, I just thought that drugs made people stupid and careless. I did my best to keep them off my stage, too.

I am a soldier. One of those people who has a strong social need to serve others regardless of the cost. One of those who, when danger manifests, runs toward it rather than away. People like me not only join the military, they become police, security, and medical professionals. And there is a social worker buried within all of us.

The threat to my friends worried me a great deal. They were blitzed out of their minds at the time and heedless of the consequences. I agonized about this, but what could I do? One night I decided I had to do something and made a phone call and then met someone in the dark of night to offer myself up as a secret soldier in the fight against this scourge. This was not just my romantic nature. I had a purpose and a hope that what I was about to do would always stay hidden and not get me killed or injured.

So, knowing the risks, I stepped up and made a deal with the cops. Leave my friends alone, and I will give you the dealers. It took some convincing but, in the end, being out of other options, they agreed and the charges against my pot-smoking friends went away. Putting students who were caught with a joint or two in jail was not going to solve the problem. The cops knew that. But they had no idea of where it was all coming from or how it was distributed. They needed me. So much that they agreed not try to supervise me and just leave me be to find out what I could. I would be on my own with no support. Which is exactly how I wanted it.

I will not describe the method by which I relayed the information I gleaned about dealers. It was a secret and shall remain so. The cops liked it because it allowed them to focus their efforts and make arrests that would result in convictions.

Not that any of them, save one Detective Lieutenant, knew who I was. There was a leak in the department—another reason the dealers eluded arrest.

One of my conditions was that I would stay in the shadows and not have to do dumb and obvious things such as actually buying drugs or using them. Given my open opposition to even marijuana that would have screamed "Narc!" to the world. My method was simpler. Just hang out and observe what went down. Listen rather than talk. Provide information, not evidence.

I was a perfect spy, already in place. Another condition I made was that my spying would not slop over into politics, especially about the war. I have a high regard for the Constitution and was not about to go in for the oppression of free expression. My politics have always been liberal. I am that rarest of all political birds: a Liberal Hawk.

When I wrote my father about my call to duty, so he would know what had happened if things went wrong, his only reply was that he hoped I wasn't doing it for selfish reasons or to get even with someone. He did not tell me not to do it and he did not tell my mother.

I acquired a Walther P38 9mm pistol with white plastic grips, which I covered with flat black cloth tape for concealment and better handling. I cut crosses in the tips of the bullets so that maximum impact could be delivered at short range. I might well have to kill someone if things got sticky and they came at me, but—as the gun culture saying goes—if it came to that, I preferred to be tried by twelve rather than carried by six.

I only carried this weapon at night, when going around looking for trouble. I had no permit because those are public records and my having one would have raised questions. Carrying the pistol would have attracted attention in the daytime, but at night it fit rather neatly in my overcoat pocket. I limited my drinking, too. I didn't want to make a mistake. That would have been really stupid. I bought an old rusty Ford station wagon for forty dollars to improve my mobility and parked it in an alley several blocks away, never bothering to change the registration. I had no privacy where I lived and it became a kind of mobile lock box. I stashed the pistol there most of the time, along with books and records I didn't want "borrowed" and never returned. There was this charming theory that property was theft and people could just take your things without so much as a "by-your-leave." Some things I just didn't want to share. My camera was always with me.

I had to work to earn the money to support that lifestyle. I bought a lot of beer for my friends. Bull sessions were also intelligence-collecting opportunities. The increased mobility allowed me to find other jobs further away and move farther afield at night after the buses stopped running.

I worked for a while at a car wash and briefly at a plant that made wooden pallets for the U.S. Army, which suddenly had lots of stuff to ship overseas. 180 nails in each one, driven by hand in a freezing-cold outside yard. I didn't keep that job long. Mostly, I was a cook.

Drugs and drink do make people stupid, and some of the lesser dealers were openly defiant of the law, advertising their wares at parties and in those all-night bull sessions at the Hamburger Hamlet and other gathering places. I was looking for them, but also for whomever was supplying them. I cultivated the patience of a duck hunter, wandering around with my camera and a long lens: taking pictures of everyone, not just the usual suspects.

I was out of the dorms by this time, having spent the summer rooming with a law student who was bemused and moralistic about the girls I brought home to photograph in the nude. It was work for my Creative Photography class and, while I looked, I never touched. There is an ethic between a photographer and a nude model that sex is not part of the deal. He was skeptical of the idea that I was doing this mostly to improve my skills. The nude is the most challenging problem in art photography and you learn by doing. The law student was about to be married and his fiancée was something of a disapproving prude. We parted on good terms, but I had to find another apartment so she could move in. I moved in with two other guys I knew slightly, neither one of whom seemed particularly interested in drugs. They were serious business students I'd met in those classes and sometimes drank beer with.

CHAPTER 8

Not even the cops really cared about marijuana. It was LSD that they saw as the real threat, and the biggest advocate for LSD was Timothy Leary, former Harvard professor and then-current cultural icon. It was his advocacy for hallucinogens that recruited me to the war on drugs. He ruined people. One of them was my best friend from high school, whom I had last seen so drug-addled that he could barely function. He'd had a golden future that was now gone. I took his fall into drugs personally because he was no longer the brilliant friend I'd known and cherished, but a zombie. I hated Timothy Leary and all he stood for.

But I didn't say much about it. I knew enough about organizations to know that the real actors would never openly sell drugs, instead manipulating the smaller fry to get the maximum advantage. I kept looking for that link and pretended criminal tendencies I did not possess. Here, a little acting training was very useful; there was always someone offering something of that kind. Opportunities to be a bad-ass abounded.

There were a couple of idiots who were stealing small balls of silver from the electroplating shop at the Collins Radio plant in Cedar Rapids. These were the left-overs weighing about a quarter pound each. Collins apparently had very poor inventory controls because they were never missed. But it was obvious what they were and where they came from. They would have to be melted down and recast into bars.

I didn't have a foundry nor did I know anyone who did. Such were my reasons for declining the deal.

That conversation and the gun in my pocket were enough to admit me to what passed for the criminal underworld in Iowa City in 1966. The standards were as low as the morals. Anyone could play. And I didn't turn the deal down entirely, but promised to keep looking for a buyer for them—for a cut of the action, of course. I obviously needed money because I was also working nights and weekends as a restaurant cook and hustling whatever photography jobs I could find.

I never got paid for being an undercover police agent, for my own safety. Funds have to be accounted for and someone in that department was dirty and working for the dealers. For that same reason I was never sworn and there was no paper on me. I was not even a "C.I.": a Confidential Informant. Nor was I willing to commit a crime so I could become one. That also struck me as supremely stupid when it was offered. It would follow me the rest of my life.

Hang around long enough, you begin to discern certain patterns and see certain relationships. It wasn't hard. I professed no interest in politics or religion and practiced active listening. After a few weeks, I began to watch one particular individual. He was pretty low-key and stood out in my grungy crowd of intellectuals and artists because he looked like a Young Republican most of the time. At first, I assumed he had some kind of job that demanded he look so straight, but he had interesting friends. They were sometimes nervous, even sweating and often seemed a bit out of it. I finally put it together. He was dealing drugs.

Sonny* was a graduate student and avowed Marxist. He was someone I met casually at parties where he would hold forth about the "coming revolution." I liked him at first because he also said many times that drug use was stupid, and reminded people that Nikita

Khrushchev had been quoted as saying that it was one of the decadent habits that the USSR would use to destroy us. In that regard, he was scornful and all for it. Most people thought he was joking, but he got my attention and I began to look carefully at him. He was thin with a narrow pinched face. In the pocket notebook where I kept track of the people I was interested in, he was labeled *R*. Or *Rat*.

He looked and dressed like a business major, sometimes even wearing a red bow tie and professorial brown tweed sports jacket with leather elbow patches. He was of medium height and had a sardonic wit. He was close to invisible. Just another graduate student and giving off this "harmless" vibe when he was actually the most dangerous man in town. It took me weeks to figure that out. I thought his Marxism was an act. And it was, something he used to hide his true nature. He was a far better actor than I would ever be and he never touched drugs.

He hung around, drinking coffee and talking trash about what he and his ilk would do when the inevitable revolution occurred. But he was willing to fence the silver balls. I was amused. This was the same guy who'd assured me that, come the Revolution, I would not be lined up against the wall and shot, but sent to a re-education camp because I wasn't really dangerous.

"So you're now a capitalist pig?" I said, laughing.

"Not at all," he rejoined smoothly. "Revolutions have to be financed and bank robberies are impractical: too much noise and attention."

So we worked out a deal. Sonny wanted bulk and a one-time deal, and at least one hundred pounds of silver to make the risk worth his while. Otherwise, no deal. I promised to talk to my guys, but specified they were only in Iowa City on weekends for the parties. They were blue collar workers, not students.

CHAPTER 9

I fell in love again, this time with Deborah*, who was both beautiful and wicked smart. She was only 18 years old and already a Junior. She spoke six languages fluently and was in the Undergraduate Poetry Workshop. I was introduced to her by Susan*, a psychology major who still lived in the dorms and was willing to date me despite being engaged to a man at another school far away. My rule about other guys did not apply to distant lovers. Susan used that big diamond ring mostly to fend off men she found unattractive. She was a serial kisser at parties. I remember the ones she exchanged with me as being extremely erotic, like eating a slightly overripe peach very slowly. She reveled in her sensuality and never minded if my hands wandered. She liked being felt up. But she also kept firm control so that anything further was at her option and discretion. She was a natural dominatrix without all the expensive gear. It was both frustrating and amusing because you knew that most of her other suitors were treated the same way—except when they weren't. Despite that diamond ring on her finger, she was quietly and systematically sleeping her way through all of the guys in our circle after swearing them to secrecy. Except me. I was teased with girlish confidences about her lovers because I was never shocked and sometimes amused. I kept these tales to myself. Discretion is the better part of valor and I wanted her friendship.

She was a very voluptuous, attractive brunette that I met browsing books at *The Paper Place*. Conversation led to coffee and that became a series of dates. She was a product of "the right kind of school" and had the unconscious upper class elegance and graceful manners that came from Money. Her family was extremely wealthy but she'd found sorority life at an upscale Ivy League college boring and transferred to Iowa to distance herself from her parents and the endless round of family obligations that imprisoned her soul. She was very smart. At parties, when she was bored, we would sometimes find a quiet corner and she would make out a little with me—but not go all the way. Why?

"I have to have one close male friend I'm not sleeping with," she said simply, over dinner one night. We had one class together and were in the same study group. I usually took her to dinner afterward. Hoping against hope, I suppose, that she would relent and let me join the queue.

"Why pick on me?"

"You're in the Drama department, so I assumed . . . "

"Jeez. Not that again!"

"Well, you're very nice. And you talk to me like I'm a person. But maybe that's the problem. You're too nice. I'm not looking for nice. It's boring."

"You're not looking for nice?"

"You know I'm engaged. He's a virgin and thinks I am, too. I do not plan to tell him otherwise, because that would end it. And we marry for life. Once married, I will not cheat and will just hope for the best. He might be great in bed, but probably not, not the way he was raised."

"So you're trying to pack a lifetime of love-making into the time left before the wedding?" I said, a bit sarcastically.

She was coolly unembarrassed. "I am. And it has been very educational. The reason I won't cheat is that most men can't satisfy me. They are too shy, too tentative. They treat me like I'm made out of glass and might break. They think of me as a real lady, but I'm quite the other thing. I like it rough. And I want lots of it, in every hole I have. That's the only way I get any relief."

I sat there, a bit stunned and more than a little aroused. It occurred to me later that she was also the biggest tease around and part of her pleasure came from denying sex to others. That it might have all been a lie. Only later did I realize that if she thought me a Queer then she had subconsciously pigeon-holed me as "one of the girls." I was part of her "circle." That explained much of what happened later and the girlish confidences she exchanged with Mark Malcas when he held court at the IMU. Both of them were pushing boundaries and both read me wrong. But I was not that sophisticated then and couldn't let it go.

"Look," I said, "I'm an actor and I can . . . "

She laughed outright. "I'm sure you can. Just not with me. But let me set you up with my friend Deborah. She's very nice, and being from New York City, very advanced. It's not an automatic thing, but she's not a virgin."

"Neither am I."

"If you say so," she smiled in a patronizing way. That was infuriating, but the problem was I did like her in other ways and wanted to stay friends. Maybe if her friend gave me a good report she would relent and let me fuck her.

It never happened, of course. Partially because Deborah was so unexpected. Petite, with a big pile of dark red hair, an hourglass body, and a face out of *The Arabian Nights*, she was not just beautiful but very intelligent, incredibly well-read, and gave me this stunned look when we first met as if I were the most attractive man she'd ever seen. And I had a similar reaction to her. Maybe it was the pheromones, but we ended up in bed the first night we met, at my apartment, with my roommates sleeping in the adjoining room with the door open. It made her shy but also very excited. She had multiple orgasms that she did not vocalize too much. She stayed the night since her dorm had a curfew hour we'd gone past, and there we were the next morning, alone in the room now, looking at each other in dazed wonder. What was this? More than just a roll in the hay, that was for sure. We had amazed each other.

It was spectacular sex, but there was more. We had been in each other's arms all night, and lazily made love again. She was able to scream a bit this time and that made her happy. I suggested breakfast. She looked at her watch and said, "I have a class." She suddenly seemed unhappy to be there, as if it were all a mistake.

She went into the bathroom and pulled herself together. I got dressed, too. She came out, smiling tentatively and said, "I will date you. But there are conditions."

"Okay. Such as?"

"I am not your girl or your honey or any of that nonsense. There will be no P.D.A. Public displays of affection. You will treat me like a lady and not do guy things to me. No pats on the ass. Not even a kiss on the cheek."

I was bemused. "Okay. I'll try to remember all that."

"If you don't, it's over."

I must have looked crestfallen because then she smiled and went to her knees in front of me. "There will be rewards for good behavior," she said as she opened my fly and took me into her mouth. I was quickly hard again. She tucked it back in and zipped me up.

"Save that for tonight," she said, grinning as she picked up her books, went to the door and down the stairs. I wondered if I had bitten off more than I could chew. Four times in less than 12 hours and now this, which would give me "blue balls" all day long.

It was, to that point, the best sex I'd ever had, but there was more there, a lot more. I was entranced, under her spell. She was definitely a Pagan.

I had classes myself. I wore my overcoat and kept it closed to conceal the massive boner she'd left me. It was agony but there was something else. I felt myself already falling in love. I had never met anyone like her. I thought her very special.

Of course, between classes and trying to write fiction for my writers' workshop class, and maintaining the social life I enjoyed for its own sake as for its utility as a cover for finding drug dealers, Deborah and I didn't have that many opportunities for lovemaking. She lived in a dorm and I had roommates. It was usually on the weekends. Weeknights usually ended long after dorm curfew at 4 a.m. in a coffee shop after an all-night bull session with other older students.

Sonny was also a regular and we had to eat to stay in the booths we occupied. The talk was challenging, about anything and everything between as many as a dozen of us. Those encounters were also exciting in a different way. They stimulated the mind instead.

Deborah and Susan and their friend Alice* were roommates at a dorm on that side of the river. Sometimes the other two would tag along when we went to a movie or a play, making me their leader and deferring modestly to me in public. I enjoyed this immensely. At parties, as the boozed flowed, the rule about public displays of affection was sometimes suspended. Susan would hold my arm tight around her waist, leaning back against me as she carried on conversations and Deb rubbed up against me like a cat. Alice was more circumspect, trying to relax but usually stiff as a board even when she wanted me to kiss her. This was a defense mechanism designed to chase away an unwanted suitor. They all pretended I was in charge. I was never fool enough to believe that, even for a minute. To keep everyone off balance I also escorted them individually and in pairs. Not that we were always all together. Susan's other liaisons, classes, and a host of other things left each of us on our own most of the time. One guy had the bad taste to offer me money to set up a date with Alice. I knocked him to the ground and kicked him in the balls. No further offers were made. Everyone heard about that.

I was taking a break from Drama and exploring my options, but I still had friends in the department and went to see their performances. I was still working shifts cooking pizza or steaks or breakfast at three very different restaurants on an "as needed" basis. An eight-hour shift was ten bucks, usually in cash.

Susan held to her "friends only" policy and Alice was too shy with men for even a long kiss. She was a scared little rabbit rather than a Playboy bunny. She had dishwater blonde-brown hair and wore bulky sweaters and black tights under a long skirt on most days. Not as pretty as she could have been with better make-up and clothing choices.

One of the straight guys in the Drama department joked that I was hogging the action after I showed up at one department party with all three of them, with all of them treating me like a boyfriend to fend off other guys. I didn't try to correct this misimpression because I hoped to convert it from a fantasy to a reality. And I enjoyed the "street cred" it generated.

I was old enough to buy booze from the State liquor store, so sometimes, when my roommates were both away for the weekend, we had our own party. We'd sit, drink, smoke, talk, and listen to my collection of jazz recordings and read poetry aloud. Some of the talk was about sex. All three girls were experimenting with Wicca and

A Perfect Spy

talked about the occult in guarded tones.

Deborah was so much more advanced than I was in sexual matters. And ideas like Open Marriage were not just discussed but more or less shouted from the rooftops. Deborah seemed to be an expert about sexual underground topics that were just beginning to emerge into the limelight. But then she was from New York City and so much more sophisticated than us rubes. She was a trailblazer, Deb was. Our willing guide to the Dark Side of Sexuality.

Deborah introduced me to Kink in a serious way. When I asked her what else I could do to please her, she smiled and said, "I like to be tied up and spanked."

"Really?"

"You can even torture me a little. Hold back. Keep me on the edge."

"You're kidding?"

"No. In here, when we're alone, you can do anything you want to me."

I had to think about that for a few moments. She was so serious about letting me use her as I would that it scared me. She wanted me to hurt her. The very idea made her breath just a little bit harder. But I knew there had to be limits.

"Like what?"

Her eyes twinkled. "Surprise me."

So I did. You can do a lot with candles, blindfolds, and ice cubes. Being tied up really excited her. She had a ready portfolio of roles she would play and a ribald imagination. She liked it all. I enjoyed the fantasy aspects of it. It is a form of theatre.

One Saturday night, my multi-partner fantasy came close to becoming a reality. We were all very drunk and the room was very hot. Deborah, because she was now in a familiar and comfortable space with her own drawer in my dresser, took off most of her clothes,

-51-

saying, "It's not anything you all haven't seen." She even took off her bra. She was small but had big, full breasts with erect nipples she displayed now with an open nonchalance.

Susan shrugged, then also disrobed and sat on a chair in an expensive black silk bra and panties as she continued to drink. She looked like Marlene Dietrich in *The Blue Angel* because she also was wearing a matching garter belt, silk stockings, and high heels. She had long elegant legs she liked to show off. Alice looked uncertain, but not wanting to be left out, reluctantly did likewise. Her cotton bra and panties didn't match, but she had a very nice, slender body with big breasts. I took my shirt and T-shirt off. Anything to oblige. Susan was quietly amused and Alice a little scared. Susan declined my request to photograph her because she looked so sexy. She couldn't risk it getting back to her future husband or her parents.

We continued to drink and talk for about an hour. I had a raging erection but just waited for something to happen. Deborah, who was about five feet tall, sat in Susan's lap, playing with her hair. They French-kissed. Alice looked distressed, burst into tears, and ran into the kitchen. Susan looked exasperated, then got up and went after her. There was murmured conversation.

Deborah shrugged, came back to me, put her hand over my groin and said, "That's a very serious condition. We'll have to do something to reduce the swelling."

And sometime after that, as Deborah and I were making love, Susan and Alice, now dressed, came back. Susan leaned over the bed and reached out to Deborah, who tried to pull her in. She smiled and backed away. "Not this time," she said. "Alice needs to go home."

Alice was still tearful, not looking at any of us. She and Susan left, and Deborah and I got back to what we were doing.

The next morning I asked Deborah to marry me. She said yes.

Susan and I had a pre-arranged date for breakfast the following Monday. When I told her that Deborah and I were now engaged, she rolled her eyes and then said, very kindly, "That's a mistake."

"Really?"

She studied the menu, not looking at me. "Being good in the sack does not make a marriage." Susan was a psychology major and held herself to have special insights into the minds of others.

"Well, of course not, but we have a lot in common. She's really smart."

"And so are you. Too smart to be that dumb. She's just using you."

I was offended. "Some friend you are."

She put the menu down and sighed. "Stop being such a Guy, Francis. It doesn't become you. Think with your brain for once and not that other big head."

Seeing my look, she added, "Yes, she told me. Rod of iron was how she put it. But that's sex, not love." She put her hand on mine, being kind again, "Look, friend, when we were leaving and she tried to pull me into bed with you both, what was your reaction?"

"Honestly. I hoped it would happen. I've always wanted you."

"And knowing what a total slut I am, would you also marry me?"

"Not if I had to take a number," I admitted.

"Well, my husband won't. Because married is married and I will be true to him. What I'm doing here with these other boys is using them for my own ends. My pleasure, not theirs, but that will stop when I am married because he will be my life. I love him, totally and completely. I won't even think about all of this. The past is past."

We were silent for a while, eating.

"Why did Alice get so upset?"

Susan looked away. "That was my fault. Deborah likes to make out with other girls. It's a provocation. And it's fun, a way to practice for the real thing. On the surface, she's just joking and fooling around. She does it in the room all the time. It's a form of aggression. Alice is in love. She was jealous."

I blinked. "Really? I didn't think she even liked me much."

Susan gave me another exasperated look. "Not with you. With Deborah."

Being in the Theatre, I should have seen that. Not my first Lesbian friend by any means, but something even more hidden in those days than its male counterpart.

"And you?"

Susan shook her head. "Friends only, like you, but if Deborah had grabbed her hand instead, Alice would have gone along just to please her. Please don't let that happen. Alice hasn't figured it out yet. She doesn't know what she is. She's a small-town girl with strict parents who would disown her if she admitted it. Don't let Deborah bully her into it. It would destroy her."

I didn't know what to say. I thought that Susan was full of herself and a little bit over the top with all of this, but I knew the dividing line between fantasy and reality and between love-making and rape even then. And Alice did seem very fragile at times.

"Okay. For you."

"Oh, please! Not for me. For Alice, and for you and Deborah, if you are serious about her. Has she asked you to tie her up yet?"

I nodded.

"That's one of the things she likes to talk about in the room when the lights are out and we're just having girl talk. She's into punishment. Low self-esteem."

"What do you mean?"

"She used to be a cutter back in New York. Look at the insides of her arms and thighs and you will see all these little white scars. Pain gets her off. She still hurts herself sometimes. When she talks to her father on the telephone, she gets very depressed and needs to relieve it. Pain makes it go away. They argue sometimes. There is something very dark going on there."

At the time I was too naïve to understand what Susan was talking about.

"You like rough sex, too, you said."

"I do. Trust me, this is something different and it puts a cloud on her heart."

She shook her head and then smiled. "Maybe I'm just being silly. Maybe you two will make a go of it. I love her as a friend and love you as a friend, but I won't sleep with either of you."

"Why not?"

"Because it's too much. I have this fantasy about having two men at the same time, and thinking about it makes me very hot, but I'd never do it, out of respect. Someone would always be left out. Three is a crowd. And that goes double for you and Deb."

I would have loved to write about this for my workshop class, but there were rules. One was no pornography and the guy in the class who'd been chastised for it had not described anything even as close to being out of the mainstream as what I was doing with Deborah and her friends. It was bad enough to be presumed Queer and I was not as brave as Mark Malcas, willing to shout my perversions to the world. This was still Iowa.

"Why do you keep a gun under your pillow?" Susan suddenly asked as we left to go to our separate classes. That surprised me, because I was always careful to hide it before our drinking parties. Guns and booze are a bad, sometimes fatal, combination. But Deborah knew I had it because I kept it under the pillow when she and I were alone together.

"I'm paranoid, and I'm doing something that might bring trouble. She told you?"

"Oh, yes. It turns her on. She thinks you're some kind of crook. That excites her, you as an outlaw. But you're not, are you?"

"No. But I can't talk about it."

There was great concern in her eyes. "Whatever it is, do be careful. I won't say a word, but you won't be able to hide it forever. It will come out."

"Not if I can help it."

"I will pray for you," she said, giving me a sisterly kiss on the cheek as we parted. That was love. As far as I know, she was able to marry the man she loved with him never learning of her true sexual nature.

CHAPTER 10

My two silver thieves eventually came back with brown gunny sacks of silver balls. They were nervous now, because that much missing silver had finally gotten someone's attention. Plant Security was on the hunt. I waited until the time was right and told Sonny that they had enough to do the deal. We were sitting at that Hamburger Hamlet close to the campus where my former roommate, Mike, was still the cook on the night shift.

"How much is there?" Sonny asked.

"They say about 530 pounds."

He pulled a large wad of bills from his back pocket, leaned over and counted it. He was careful not to let anyone else see what he was doing.

"Three thousand dollars. Not a penny more," he said after a moment.

"That's not much, considering," I said.

"Considering what?" Sonny smiled. He had perfect white teeth, like a movie star.

"The risk."

"Shit, I'm the one who's taking the risk here. All they had to do was steal it. I have to carry it to Chicago, get it melted down, and then sell it. Silver is at a dollar twenty-eight an ounce. Not much margin. I wouldn't bother if I didn't have to go there anyway."

I nodded. "When and where?"

He gave me a time and place the following night. Finishing his coffee, he said, "I have a class," then picked up his briefcase and left. I stayed to finish the hamburger I'd ordered. Mike came over with the coffee pot and topped off my cup. He leaned over and said quietly, "You should be careful of that guy."

I looked up because he was uncharacteristically serious now. "Why?"

"He's into some bad shit. You hear about that junkie who OD'd in our bathroom last Saturday?"

I nodded. It had been in both the city and student newspapers. Dead students attracted attention.

"Friend of his. Same department and both of them are teaching assistants. You think he'd be a bit upset, but it didn't faze him. Not a tear or moment of regret. He meets a lot of people here and some of them look really strung out."

"I don't know him that well."

Mike stared at me a long moment. "So you're some kind of crook now, too?" I could see the disappointment in his eyes.

"Nope. Just looking for characters for my fiction. He's an interesting guy."

Mike looked around. "If you say so," he said after a moment and went back to the grill. He avoided me after that, suddenly a stranger. Being diabetic, he couldn't drink, and he was as appalled by what drugs were doing to the local community as I was.

The silver thieves showed up, with their booty in the trunk of their car, and insisted I go to the meet with them. It was pouring rain and very cold; we all got thoroughly soaked. Sonny never showed. After three hours we went looking for him, first checking a number of parties he might be at and then ending up at that same Hamburger Hamlet where he usually hung out. And there he was, sitting calmly in the back booth with a couple of other guys. They were jocks, football players.

I tagged them as muscle. He's brought protection for some reason. Something else was going down that had nothing to do with the deal I'd set up. I was still pissed.

We advanced on him. "Where were you?" I said, angry now.

He smiled. "Excuse me?"

"We had an appointment," I said, trying to stay calm. My hand was gripping the Walther P38 in my right overcoat pocket and I was ready to shoot him just for making me look bad to those two fools. One of the jocks looked at me and started to get up. Sonny motioned him to sit back down.

"I don't recall that," he said smoothly. "This is my study group. We've been here all night, talking about Ernest Hemingway."

"What about him?" I asked tightly.

"Well, with all of that swagger, was he actually a Queer? Was that why he blew his head off instead of drinking himself to death? He suddenly realized it and couldn't live with himself?"

I just stared at him a moment. He was winding me up with the talk about Queers. Trying to make me go away. I took a deep breath and relaxed my grip on the pistol. He was winding me up but there was something more. He was tense and his eyes moved back and forth more than usual. He was expecting trouble and not just from me. What had I stumbled into? I tried to get myself under control with a breathing exercise. But I still needed to get my deal done.

"It's an interesting question," I said. "Can we join you?" There was room enough in the booth for six. It was an implied threat, but Sonny didn't blink and just gestured a welcome. The two jocks looked a little surprised but started to make room. Between them. Not good. It would give them a tactical advantage.

My two silver thieves looked at each other, very confused. This was out of their range. They weren't smart enough to understand the situation but possessed of a kind of animal cunning that told them the deal had gone sour.

"We've got to get back to C.R.," one of them said.

Now I had to worry that they would insist I buy the stolen silver. I had neither the money nor the inclination. They might threaten violence, but knew I was carrying the pistol and knew how to use it. They were justifiably pissed off. I didn't blame them.

"Excuse me," I said to Sonny. "Let me see my friends off. I'll be right back."

"Can we get you anything?" Sonny said, watching me and especially my right arm very carefully. That told me he was armed, too.

"A cup of coffee and some soup. I'm chilled to the bone."

He relaxed. "Sure," he said. I walked out with the two thieves, who had parked the car with the stolen silver in the trunk right outside. It was low on the rear tires from the weight.

"Hemingway was a Queer?" one of them asked, openly confused and upset by the notion.

"It's just a theory," I assured him.

"So what now," the other one said. "What do we do with it?"

"Put it back?"

"We can't. We got fired last week."

"For stealing? Why are you still walking around free?"

"No. They found grass in our lockers during a shakedown inspection. They don't call the cops on you, but you're gone the same day. They mail you your last check."

That interested me. "Why didn't they call the cops? It's a felony."

"There's too much of it. Half the night shift is high most of the time. They don't want the cops in because they have Federal contracts that would go away. They look the other way most of the time, until there's a safety violation and then they're all over it. Wasn't just us who got fired. About a dozen other guys. It will put a real crimp in production since they were on the line."

He looked around, a bit desperate. "Five hundred pounds of fucking silver. You know how much work that was? Shit! Now what do we do?"

Crime is hard, I thought to myself. I tried to smooth it over. "Maybe, if you just wait a bit. . . ."

"Fuck that. If they do an audit, that much will show up as missing and they will call the cops. What do we do with it?"

"Get rid of it. Bury it someplace or throw it in the river." I was out of patience with them. "But he's not going to buy it now."

"Why not?"

"I don't know. Maybe he heard something, or he just got nervous. The guy is like a wild animal in the forest. He senses danger, he runs."

They looked at each other. One of them stuck his hand out. "No hard feelings, Pal. You did your best." I felt considerable relief that they didn't blame me. They were not really bad guys, just trying to make a little extra money and get ahead. Clever, but not smart enough to think it all the way though.

"You get caught," I said, "I never heard of you. I don't know you."

They just nodded, got in the car and drove away. I never saw them again.

I walked back inside. Sonny was by himself now, and there was a cup of hot coffee and a steaming bowl of chicken noodle soup waiting for me. I sat down and tucked in. Sonny was watching me very carefully.

"Sorry for any inconvenience," he said at last.

"You should be."

"Were you really going to shoot me?"

"Only in the kneecaps."

He laughed loudly. I joined in. It broke the tension. The truth was that we were becoming friends of a sort. We enjoyed talking to each other and he was beginning to relax around me. He shoved a small brown envelope across the table at me.

I put down my spoon and stared at it. "What's that?"

"Nickel bag. But for you, on the house." Five dollars worth of marijuana.

The first one is always free, I thought.

"Thanks, but no thanks. You know I don't do that stuff."

"Your girlfriend does. Take it for her."

"I'm trying to get her off of it."

He swept the envelope off the table and put it in his pocket, as smoothly as any stage magician.

"Good luck with that."

"What do you mean?" I asked, offended now.

"Chick has serious problems. She's really in love with you and there you are with your little harem, fucking her two friends too."

I stared at him. Where the fuck had that come from?

He leaned forward. "We were talking earlier about Hemingway overcompensating for being Queer with all of his man's man bullshit, but you're just as bad. Three girls? It's wretched excess."

"Well, I didn't plan it. It just happened. It was Deborah's idea. Really."

"Sure. Susan told me all about it."

"When?"

"Last week. It was my turn to fuck her and I didn't think Pat* would mind."

Pat was his girlfriend. She was that new thing called a "flower child," a hippie, and free love was part of that. I knew her because she also modeled in the nude for the art department. She had posed for me a few times at three dollars an hour as I tried to emulate the kind of artistic nudes done by great photographers like Edward Weston. She was totally comfortable in her own skin and loved being naked, outdoors or in. You could barely tell that she had two small children of her own to care for. No stretch marks.

"Did she? Mind, I mean?"

"After all the free love bullshit she's spouted? How could she? But Susan set her off. She called her a real bitch. It's class resentment, of course. The real term is 'rich bitch.' College girls should not wear real pearls."

"And what did Susan say?"

"Back at you and at least she didn't parade around naked, like some kind of goddess. Called her a whore."

"Susan? Susan called Pat a whore?"

Sonny and I both suppressed a grin at the irony.

"Because she takes money for the modeling. Free love is supposed to be free."

"That's completely different. And it's hard work, posing. She earns that money."

"So you and Pat never . . . ?"

"Of course not. It's not about that. Look but don't touch."

"I'll bet you still got a boner," he said slyly.

I think I actually blushed.

"Okay," I said, "You've got me there. She's a very attractive girl."

Sonny bore in, with a mean grin. "And what's the difference between that and a stripper out at the Sportsman's Lodge in Coralville?"

"Well, there's no dancing, no drinking, and no tipping. The stripper is better paid."

"So, a capitalist would say she should do that instead?"

"No. She gets welfare for her kids and they like to mess with her. They threatened to take them away for the modeling. She had to get a note from the Art Department saying it's a regular student job. The other modeling she only does for those she knows and trusts, and only for cash."

Sonny looked suddenly very tired. He sighed.

"I can grok that. I offered to help her out. She refused. Very proud. Doesn't want to be "kept." So the 'whore' accusation really cut deep."

"Susan's no one to talk," I observed.

"She said she's a slut. Not in it for the money."

"A distinction without a difference," I said. "And she's from Money. Never had to struggle."

"Another one for the re-education camp," Sonny said. "Too pretty to shoot. She would come out of that a real terror. There's no one more virtuous than a reformed whore."

"Or slut."

Sonny nodded. "It's very political, you know. They're all feminists. And part of a witches' coven that dances naked in the woods when the moon is full. You believe that?"

"Sure," I said. "I knew some of those girls growing up in California. Witches don't scare me. I'm a bit that way myself."

He smiled at me but his eyes were serious. "You know, with you I never know where the truth ends and the bullshit begins."

"I'm an actor. Bullshit is my stock-in-trade."

"I know. But it worries me."

I looked outside. The sun was coming up and the rain had abated. I was dry and warm again.

"Gotta go," I said, and got up. I had a class but went home to sleep instead. I really liked Sonny. He was easy to be around and interesting to talk to. We were becoming friends. Yet I was also very determined to land him a long stretch in prison. And Deborah was the reason why. Marry in haste and repent in leisure, they say. The same is true of engagements. We were still pretty quiet about that and there was no ring yet, but I had fallen hard. I was completely and deeply in love with the little bitch and she had problems I didn't know how to solve. I wanted to save her from herself; a fool's errand if there ever was one.

And that was my grudge against Sonny. He enabled her self-destruction. He'd sold her some grass two weeks before. Susan told me that her purchase had been sparked by another fight on the telephone with her father. What the situation was, no one knew and Deborah wouldn't say, except that she had a scholarship and her other expenses were covered by her grandmother. He kept trying to pull her back to New York. It made her unhappy and while she liked booze well enough, it made her agitated and loud when she wanted to be calm.

It was not like Sonny introduced her to grass there. That had actually been Bobby*, a short, scrawny local kid with bad acne and hygiene who was one of his dealers. Sonny seldom sold directly to anyone. He was management, not labor, and flying so far below the radar that, until I tipped them off, the cops assumed he was a rather straight-laced graduate student in English. He was actually working on a PhD. He looked way too straight to be a dealer. And he was almost invisible. Never at the apartment he rented and got his mail at the post office. Rented a car when he needed one, rather than own anything with a license plate that could be traced if it showed up too many times in the wrong place. My little notebook had the numbers of half a dozen cars I'd seen him driving. All from the local Avis franchise.

He was not in the drug scene. He didn't even use! But he sold everything, and to anybody, but always at a remove. Over a beer at a local bar, he bragged to me how he'd sold some "Iowa grass" to naïve kids from Parsons College. Being temporarily short of product, he'd taken a pound of lawn clippings, rolled it in paregoric, and bagged it up with some leftover stems and leaves from the bottom of his marijuana storage bin. Three hundred dollars he charged them for this mess.

I have to admit, I laughed my ass off when he told the story. It was *Schadenfreude*. It probably made them sick as Hell and he'd cheated them big time in the bargain. But it was a one-time thing. He actually took pride in his product, like any good businessman. Which, by his reckoning, was all he was. He liked Deborah, so when she dragged me out one night to find a dealer because she was new in town and didn't know any, he broke his own rule and just sold her one of those brown envelopes he was holding for his crew. She was in a class he helped teach about Chaucer. He liked her.

As to where he got his drugs, well, Chicago was a five-hour drive away. At various times he mentioned doing library research at the University of Chicago. That was located on the South Side, close to all kinds of dealers in the Black communities. On the North Side was Northwestern, close to Old Town and New Town. Plenty of connections there . . . and he went to Chicago once or twice a week. No one had the resources to follow him. When I got into Military Intelligence I learned how many people are required for an effective tail. Following him from Iowa City along Interstate 80 would have been a fool's errand, even if that old beater I drove could have made it.

And there was never enough for the cops to get a warrant for a search of one of those cars. Suspicion is not a crime.

CHAPTER 11

When Deborah bought that grass from Sonny, we walked back to my place. Once upstairs, she spread her purchase out on a dinner plate, then scooped it up and put it back in the envelope except for some that she rolled in a joint. He had given her a complimentary package of ZigZag papers.

"This is good shit," she said, "No stems or leaves." She started to light up.

"Hey," I said, "You can't do that here! My landlady will evict us. She's already warned my roommates twice."

Deborah stared at me with her big dark brown eyes and sighed. "You're not being a very good boyfriend, again."

"Sorry," I said, "But that old bitch comes by every morning to check and sniff the curtains. Midterms are coming up. I can't move and neither can the other guys. Where would we go?"

"Fine!" she said, tucking the joint and the grass into her bra. She got up. I started to, and she said, "You stay here and think about this. You've let me down again."

"Again? When was the first time?"

"Last night. You know how." Her back stiff with real anger, she went to the door and down the stairs. I was perplexed. I smoked cigars, which the landlady also complained about but was no real cause of action for an eviction. I could have lit one to cover the smell from her joint . . . or would it be joints? She was a creature of excess. One of anything was never enough for her. She liked being controlled in bed and hated it when we were together in public. What had set her off this time?

And then it came to me. The previous night we'd made love and she was imaging what might lie beyond a simple spanking. This was not my thing and, try as I might, I didn't really care for it. Having her bound and helpless was another matter because I could give her some intense pleasure. We could improvise, and she could be the little helpless maiden in the clutches of a cruel villain, or she could pretend to be a naughty schoolgirl. Harmless enough play. But it wasn't enough that night. She popped out of bed, nude, bent over, grabbed her ankles and demanded that I beat her ass with my belt. Hard.

I got out of bed, stripped the belt from my jeans, and stood behind her.

"Close your eyes," I said. "You can't see it coming or you'll flinch. And this is going to hurt you more than it hurts me."

She nodded and closed them tightly. I made her wait for it, trying to figure a way not to do it. At least not more than once. I swung the belt a couple of times to get a feel for it and then laid one hard across both cheeks. Her eyes and mouth popped open and her expression haunts me to this day. It was so much more than what she'd expected. It hurt her both physically and emotionally and I was afraid I'd really damaged her. She was amazed by real pain.

I took her in my arms. "How did that feel?"

"Fantastic," she lied, with tears streaming from her eyes. "Please, sir, may I have another?"

"No," I said. "No, I love you and this is not what I want to do to you when we're alone."

She collapsed into tears. It was my first time with a scene like that and I missed several clues. She was in a very dark place. Probably a victim of sexual child abuse, something that was never discussed at all back then. Full of self-hatred and rage. She had herself a good cry and dropped off to sleep. The next morning it was like the whole thing had never happened except for the welt on her ass. I was confused.

She avoided me for a couple of days, withholding her favors as punishment. Then she was back. I was really confused now.

The only person I could talk to about this was Susan who, it turned out, knew a thing or two about the darkness. She lent me her copy of *The Story of O* and the Marquis de Sade's *The 120 Days of Sodom and Philosophy in the Bedroom*.

I returned them a few days later.

"What did you think?"

"Really sick stuff."

"You didn't like it?"

"No, I did. It turned me on a little, but that's not how I want to treat my wife or my girlfriend." I looked at her condescending smile and felt like hitting her.

"It's not something you do every day," she said after a moment. Looking around the restaurant we were in to make sure she was not observed, she hiked up her skirt up. She almost never wore slacks or jeans. Always a lady-like conservative skirt set and blouse. Usually with a garter belt and stockings. Today they were missing and she was black and blue. Bruises everywhere on her thighs and pelvis. She quickly pulled the skirt back down.

I was just stunned. "Who did that to you?" I said, growing angry.

"Take it easy, Cowboy. It was my idea. I asked for it. Literally, in so many words."

That took my breath away. I just stared at her for several seconds.

"Why, for God's sake, would you let anyone do that to you?"

Her superior manner went away and she looked down, now a bit ashamed. "So I could feel something. So I'd know I'm alive."

I shook my head.

"You want to know who? Sonny. I finally let him have me, but he had to earn it."

"He did a hell of a job," I said sarcastically.

"He did," she replied. "I came so many times I lost count."

She ran her finger slowly around the rim of her beer glass and couldn't meet my eyes. "You want to know why I know so much about Deborah's troubles? It's because they're also my troubles. I know what happens to young girls when Daddy comes into their room late at night and wants more than just a kiss goodnight."

"That happened to you?"

She nodded. "And Deb and Alice. It's our common denominator. But we're hardly alone. It happens everywhere, usually in very religious families you'd never suspect."

She put her hand over mine. "Don't be so sad. I enjoyed the whole thing. You can't blame Sonny."

"But I do. What kind of man does that to a woman. It's disgusting."

"Well, he's a sociopath, you know. Other people aren't real to him. He manipulates them for his own ends. It's all about him."

"And you approve of that?"

"Only where it serves me. Maybe I'm one, too, except I do feel others' pain and anger. But I used him as much as he used me."

"And you'll do it again?"

"No. Not with him. Probably not with anyone. I just wanted to know what it feels like to fall into the hands of an angry god. One with no mercy. Now I know. That's enough."

She was cool enough.

" 'I am a stranger in a strange land,' " I said.

"Sure you are. Don't be too hard on Deb. She's still figuring it out, just like the rest of us. She'll be okay."

"I'm not so sure."

"Still going to marry her?"

"I love her, so I'll probably work it out with her. Try anyway."

For once she had nothing more to say. She finished her beer, dimpled a smile at me, then got up, took her purse and her school books, and left, pausing only to kiss me on the cheek. I sat there, ordered more beer and tried to get drunk.

CHAPTER 12

I didn't see Deborah or Susan for several days after that. I was behind in my classes and trying to catch up. I was also on academic probation, and if my grade point average dropped low enough I'd lose my draft deferment. The war in Vietnam had become ours rather than South Vietnam's. There was a lot of fear. An undercurrent of propaganda about how bad and dangerous the war was became pervasive. It was being orchestrated by the SDS and articles expressing their viewpoint appeared almost daily in *The Daily Iowan* to balance out the mainstream media coverage. People scoffed when I said I was willing to go—until I explained that my father was an Army officer. Then they felt sorry for me.

One morning at the Iowa Memorial Union this one guy stood up, loudly announced his name, said he was against the "illegal" war in Vietnam and then announced he would not be drafted. He set fire to his draft card. No one really paid any attention because people did weird stuff all the time at the IMU. Certainly no one cheered or spoke out in support. We didn't realize that we had witnessed the opening shot of a second enemy front, one that would ultimately defeat us—the war at home.

How? Because SDS jumped on the opportunity and a guy named Steve Smith later burned his draft card in front of a large crowd at a Soundoff Soapbox event. He was arrested and his troubles dominated the news for several months until he was convicted and given three years' probation. This also kept the war on the front page, too. Stories about battles like Ia Drang where the First Cavalry fought a superior enemy force to a standstill ran side-by-side with those about rising resistance to the Draft. A Draft that would send young men into battle against their will. Some of them, and their families, began to seek ways to avoid such a fate. They considered it a death sentence.

Susan was absent for a week or two and unwilling to explain. Deborah told me that she'd gotten pregnant and had to arrange an abortion, which were still illegal in Iowa. Her plight was hardly a surprise, but she managed it. F. Scott Fitzgerald once said, "The rich are very different from you and me." To which Ernest Hemingway rejoined, "Yeah, they have more money."

Whatever had happened, her family pulled together for her and took care of it. No back alleys for her. A nice surgical clinic at night, followed by a week's recovery in the Bahamas. Her fiancé was left clueless. "Female trouble" covered a lot of ground and he was too squeamish to inquire into the exact causes of her sudden illness. It had been covered by the removal of a perfectly healthy appendix at the hospital.

Deborah decided to forgive me for not being mean to her and we resumed our relationship. We went to parties some nights. Drinking and talking with our friends. Finals were coming and we had to study. She decided that marijuana was a study aid and kept trying to get me to try it, while I was still looking around trying to figure how Sonny's whole operation worked and who was involved. The little notebook was filling up. I had an excellent memory so I only wrote in it when I was alone. Usually in a stall in the men's room.

Deborah was very bright and funny a lot of the time, but there was a part of her that was determined to die. One night she really shocked me by asking me to take my gun and kill her. I refused, of course, and demanded that she get some help. Student health had shrinks on duty for just that kind of thing. I was more careful with my pistol after that, recognizing that she might use it to do herself harm.

Where did Sonny keep his drugs? This was a question often relayed to me by my cut-out with the police. There was a lot more LSD in town and some students couldn't handle it. There was a rumor that someone had stepped out of a fourth-floor window at one of the dorms and fallen to his death. That was hushed up as an accident. A couple of others had psychotic breaks and ended up in the local mental hospital. Closer to home, one of my roommates dropped acid and decided to finally come out.

"I am a homosexual," he solemnly declared to me one night.

Geez, I thought. Why tell me? What was I supposed to do about it?

"Okay," I said, "Glad we cleared that up. You want another beer?"

I was more worried about him repeating his acid trip. The popular and received wisdom was that you had to keep a lot of Vitamin B-6 around, or Thorazine in a hypodermic, as a first-aid measure for a bad trip, but no one knew where to get that last or if it would actually work. We were suddenly in the midst of a public health crisis. I blamed Sonny, but he didn't care and I could not berate him. Rather I stuck to him like glue as he bragged about his operations, leaving out the essential details of where and when transactions would occur. I was willing to break cover to nail his sorry ass, but he was too clever. He was also arrogant. When one of his underlings expressed worry about the "Feds," he confirmed he had someone inside at the police department and was being tipped off.

"Besides, there are no Feds around here. I'd smell them a mile away."

He was looking directly at me when he said it. My years of poker playing came in handy then. I didn't say or do anything to make him worry about me.

I was out by myself one night, just looking around. Sonny was never at his place, but suddenly the lights were on and here was activity. I wondered if he was clever enough to hide his stash in plain sight. There still wasn't enough information to get a search warrant. I was on a crusade now. I wanted very badly to see him arrested for something, anything, even a parking ticket. I skipped classes and ran short of sleep.

And the whole thing with Deborah broke apart one morning after I'd been out all that night chasing this ghost. I came back to the apartment at six a.m., opened the door, and heard a woman's voice in the next room. It was Deb, and she was in bed—not with my other roommate but with Bobby the drug dealer. It was too much! I was suddenly blind with anger. I stood over them, furious.

Deb looked up at me, confused, chagrined, and then blushing with shame. She grabbed her clothes and ran into the bathroom. Bobby swung his legs over the side of the bed and looked up at me with a sick, miserable expression. He was very hung over. I was toying with the Walther, turning it over in my hands.

"Aw, come on, Hamit. You're not going to shoot me. You're too pure for that."

"Don't be so sure," I said coldly.

"For her? That little cunt?"

"Dangerous ground, Bobby. You're talking about the woman I love."

"Then I feel sorry for you. You think this was my idea? You going to shoot anyone, shoot her," He shook his head miserably, obviously not caring if I did shoot him.

That decided me.

"Get dressed and get your stuff and get out of my place."

I waved the barrel of the P38 to emphasize my point. Grumbling, he hurried to comply. I stuck the gun in my pocket and walked him out. On the landing, he seemed remorseful.

"Hey, man. I'm sorry it went down like this," He stuck out his hand. "No hard feelings."

"None at all," I replied, as I took his hand, twisted his arm behind his back and propelled him down two flights of stairs. He crashed nosily at the bottom and, bloody now, stumbled out into the street.

"You're crazy, man!" floated back up as I walked back into the apartment to find Deborah standing there, shaking with fear.

"Get your stuff," I said, "and get out." My voice was very cold. And then I watched her do it, my heart breaking but my face hard. After she left, I sat, drinking and crying for a long time.

CHAPTER 13

That wasn't the end of it, of course. We still ran into each other, but the first time it happened, the look in my eyes had her trembling and tearful with remorse. She was with Susan at the time, and Susan looked at me, both alarmed and angry.

She didn't want to take sides but she already had. It was Alice who became the go-between to try and patch things up. Not a surprise, when I thought about it. She was devoted to Deborah and would do anything for her. She asked me to take her to a student film showing. I obliged her because I didn't want to be alone. Of course, the audience was packed with Drama students and faculty. Our being together caused a low buzzing sound and a couple of wisecracks that we both ignored.

One short film caused Alice to grab my hand tightly. It was in vivid color and showed a man's pelvis and bare ass apparently slowly pumping himself into a woman's bare hips and legs, intertwined. It was not bold enough to show actual penetration; by today's standards it would look very tame. It sent a huge shock through the audience, which became very silent. It was breathtaking. Literally. Nothing like this had been seen before at Iowa. Yet it was not pornography, but art. Groundbreaking. Alice was amazed.

Afterward, we went for coffee. She was bright and cheerful, trying to jolly me out of my gloom. It worked a little. Finally, she looked at me shyly, and said, "Deb's really sorry, you know, about the whole thing."

"I am sure she is," I said, getting pissed off again at the indignity of being cuckolded in my own place by that little, ugly, scrawny shit Bobby, whom she would ordinarily not have given the time of day to. "I don't want to talk about it."

Alice was silent for a long time as I stared past her out into the street.

"Would you do something for me?" she asked suddenly.

"What?"

"Teach me how to make love?"

"You don't know how?"

"Not with a man. Deb and Susan showed me a few things, but the way Deb bragged about you, I know it's not the same. I don't even have orgasms with them. The whole thing bewilders and embarrasses me."

"And what do you want me to do?"

"I don't know. That's the problem. I don't know what I don't know. I'm a virgin."

"That wasn't what I heard, and I also heard that you really prefer other girls."

"I do. That's very true. I dream about Deb, even when she's with you making crazy monkey love."

I laughed out loud. "What?"

Alice blushed. "That's what she called it. But don't you think I should try it once with a man, just to be sure?"

"Why me?"

"Because you are kind and decent and won't hurt me too bad."

That touched my heart just a bit. "I won't hurt you at all," I said softly.

"But it's supposed to hurt," she said, "When you break the hymen."

I looked around, making sure no one else was listening. "So your father never . . . "

She blushed again. "All the time, but he always used the back way, so I wouldn't get pregnant. I'm intact."

Well, I thought, there's virginity and then there's virginity. What could I do but take her back to my place and show her what she wanted? And what she wanted was tenderness. I insisted on leaving the lights on. I wanted to look at her. Her big breasts turned out to be falsies. She had very little up there, mostly big, very sensitive nipples. Neither roommate was there, and she was so shy that I had to undress first and give her a guided tour of my body. Gradually I got her clothes off. We lay together naked and went from there, very slowly, her body shaking when I entered her.

"So it's good?" I asked the question no man ever should, of a woman in bed.

She nodded.

"Thank you," she said. "Very nice."

"So you'll give men a try?"

"Maybe. Does it matter that I was thinking of Deb and not you when I came?"

I looked at her eyes. There was no deception there. She was not joking with me.

"Hey, whatever works," I said, hiding my dismay.

Cuckolded again. By the same girl.

I was still hard inside her. Alice suddenly wrapped her legs around my waist, pulling me deeper in.

"Mmmm. I like this," she said, moving her hips slightly. "Makes me feel full."

"You're welcome. Are you using any birth control?"

"The pill."

That was a relief. Not an ironclad guarantee against pregnancy. It hadn't helped Susan in the end. But then, Susan had screwed so many guys that she'd lost track. No idea of who the father might be. Alice started moving her hips again.

"Come on," she said. "Your turn."

And soon it was. She was very sweet, but I wasn't going to continue seeing her. Doing that would serve neither of us. "Very nice" was a rather tepid response for my efforts. I wanted Deborah back and Alice was there, in a weird way, to make peace between us. Offering herself up as a gift or sacrifice.

It might have worked, too, had not someone taken a shot at me two nights later.

CHAPTER 14

The bullet whizzing close to my ear was a wake-up call. There was a sound like a firecracker popping off in the distance and suddenly my pistol was in my hand. I worked the action to load a round and make it easier to fire, while ducking for cover away from the orange glow of the sodium-vapor streetlight overhead. There was another shot and the splat of a bullet hitting the wall behind me. I had the shooter located now and, using the two-handed grip, fired off three rounds in his general direction. Very loud they were. Lights came on in the apartments above. There was a scrambling sound as he retreated further into the bushes he was using as cover and a distant wail of a siren as the cops rolled to investigate.

The last thing I wanted was to have to explain all this or why I carried a pistol at night. I would become a matter of record. I would be exposed. I put the pistol back in my pocket and ran away, down an alley away from downtown and didn't stop for several blocks. I could see the red and blue reflections from the lights on top of the police car only dimly from where I stopped. I was close to my car, it was 4 a.m., and I drove out to Coralville to work the early shift at the pancake house. I had a lot to think about.

Winston Churchill, writing of his experiences as a young war correspondent in the Boer War, said, "Nothing in life is so exhilarating as to be shot at without result." So it was with me that morning, as I helped cook breakfast for more than 200 people, laughing and joking with the other cooks and the waitresses, moving up and down the big grill, cracking eggs right along with the jokes and flipping pancakes. It was an endorphin high and one I didn't think about much after. After the shift was over and I was sitting in the back, out of my cook whites and now sober again, eating the free meal that was a perk of the job, I began to think hard about what had happened and what I should do about it.

The answer was nothing. The Detective Lieutenant I provided information to was supposed to be the only one who knew who I was and what I was doing. He and I never met but used a cut-out. But someone had made me or suspected me or just didn't want me around. I'd been standing in the clear. With better aim, they would have killed me or put me out of action. So maybe it was meant as a warning.

It amazed me how calm and dispassionate I was about this. I felt no panic at all, then or later. The prospect of being killed didn't bother me nearly as much as the idea of killing someone else and having to explain it. And it was that last part that worried me. Killing was easy. It was the explanation that was dangerous. The wrong one would land me in prison.

I'd gone around looking pretty tough for weeks, exhibiting a "don't fuck with me" attitude that some found intimidating and others found sexy. But it was not toughness or being *macho* that made me decide not to tell anyone about the incident. It was the cold logic of the situation. They would pull me out and put me in protective custody—and I wasn't done yet. Not by half!

So who had told them I was undercover and would they try again? Bobby? He certainly had reason enough. I'd broken his collarbone and a few other things. He couldn't complain because he'd have to explain why I'd done it. But the local grapevine reported him in jail, popped by a "kiddie cop" from Des Moines at the local high school for selling drugs there. The cop, who looked 15, was several years older. The judge posted a very high bail because of the LSD Bobby was carrying. Marijuana was nothing. It grew wild in ditches along every road in Iowa, a souvenir of efforts to grow hemp to make rope during World War II. LSD was the real threat, the thing that put fear into people's hearts for their children. Bobby was looking at five years in state prison and not even his politically-connected family could save him. To cut his time, he rolled over on some of Sonny's other dealers, who were picked up and put in jail.

But Sonny was nowhere to be found. Bobby had rolled on him, too, but he'd gone to ground. Yet, drugs continued to be sold.

With that in mind, and a fresh edict to find Sonny so he could be arrested and prosecuted, I wandered into the Iowa Memorial Union. Mark Malcas was there, as usual holding court and being flamboyant and outrageous.

"Hello, Darling," he shouted when he saw me, "I hear you've been very naughty."

Mark liked to do that to his straight male friends, just to get a rise. He never got one from me, which might have caused the misperception that I was a very closeted Queer instead. We were friends. I liked him for himself so I never shied away from him.

He patted the brown faux leather seat next to him.

"Come, sit," he said, "We must dish."

Seeing that he was by himself, I asked, "Where are your husband and your wife?"

He pouted. "Las Vegas. They ran off together and got married. Can you believe it? They didn't even invite me. I mean, you think you know people. . . ." He was almost in tears.

I sat next to him and he dropped the act. Leaning over, he whispered, "What have you been up to, Francis? There's a rumor going around that you're really not who you say you are."

"Who am I, then?"

"A narc? Some kind of undercover cop?" He looked worried now because I'd seen him smoking pot many times at parties. "I mean, you just don't seem the type."

"Well, I wouldn't, would I? Who has been saying this?"

"An unimpeachable source. Your recent lady love, Deborah. Except that Hell hath no fury like a woman scorned, and she's said other things that don't add up."

"Such as?"

"You raped Alice?"

I shook my head. "Anyone ask Alice about that?"

"She won't say. Just looks embarrassed and changes the subject. So did you?"

"It wasn't rape. She asked me to pop her cherry. You know me—anything to help out a friend. But keep that to yourself."

He pursed his lips. "I'm sorry, sweetheart. That makes no sense at all. Everyone knows that Alice is ga-ga for the luscious Deborah, who goes both ways since she met you."

He stared at me expectantly. He actually was capable of being discreet but also the biggest gossip hound around. I had to be careful what I said, lest he shout it to the world.

"Can I trust you to keep this quiet?"

"Absolutely."

I took a deep breath. "She was trying to patch it up between Deb and me."

"Odd way to do it, Deborah is furious with her."

I shrugged. "Revenge is sweet. Revenge sex is sweeter. You know why I kicked Deb out?"

"I heard that you beat the crap out of poor little Bobby and then the cops busted him for dealing."

"I caught her in bed, at my place, with the little shit, but one had nothing to do with the other. Bobby did that last to himself by selling at the high school. There are rules."

Mark shook his head, "It's all too complicated for little old me. You can't tell the players without a program. Quite a mess you've made."

"I had help."

"That you did," he sighed. "So this other thing about you being a narc is just something Deb made up to get even?"

I looked away, not answering. The penny finally dropped.

"Oh, shit!" he whispered. "Oh, God, how could you?"

I patted his hand. "You have nothing to fear. No one wants users. There are too damn many of you. It's the dealers that are the target, so we can kill it at the source."

He laughed bitterly. "You're a fool, you know. You can't spoil this party. There are drugs everywhere."

"And people are dying because of it."

"Let 'em, and leave the rest of us alone," he said, showing an unexpected libertarian streak. He drew himself up, tearful now. "I'm going to have to ask you to leave now."

I got up. Mark shook his head. "This just really breaks my heart. I don't know you anymore." This was not his usual self-dramatizing. I'd lost his friendship. I nodded. Got to my feet and moved on. He was suddenly too angry to even look at me.

I saw Deborah and Susan coming in together through the glass doors some distance away. I started walking toward them.

"I'm very disappointed in you," Mark shouted after me, using that high feminine voice he favored.

The two girls were talking and I was on them before they noticed me.

I cleared my throat. Deborah turned, saw me and turned pale. Susan bit her lip.

I was very quiet and calm.

"I understand you've been telling lies about me?"

"Oh, my God," Susan said, her voice soft and scared, "The look on your face."

Deborah couldn't meet my eyes. She looked down like a naughty school girl—a real one, not a sex fantasy. She began to shiver just a bit.

"I'm sorry," she began, "But you were so mean to me the other night and you really hurt Bobby, I just . . . " her voice trailed off.

"What?"

She couldn't answer.

"Actions have consequences, Deb. Someone took a shot at me last night. I might have been killed."

Her looked up, her face full of shock and dismay. Her lips trembled.

"I just wanted to pay you back," she protested, "I didn't think . . . "

"You sure didn't." I was getting really angry now. Susan hugged herself protectively. She had never seen me like this.

"But who would believe that? You're not . . . "

"That's the problem, Deborah. It is true. I'm a cop." I said this in a very low voice. Her eyes went wide with the shock of it. She stood there, staring at me, trying to take it in, stunned to silence. Then she bent over and threw up. A lot.

Susan recoiled, disgusted. "Now look at what you've done."

"Stay away from me. Both of you!" I said and then walked off. I looked back and Susan was trying to help Deborah to a couch. There was vomit spreading all over the marble floor. People came running up to help to help, and Susan was covering, saying something about food poisoning.

CHAPTER 15

I stayed the night at a cheap dingy white motel in Coralville and slept with the P38 in my hand. That took all of my spare cash and couldn't continue. I had classes. The weather was cold enough for an overcoat, so now I carried my pistol all the time and hoped no one would notice. It took all of my minimal acting skills to get through the day.

Whoever had shot at me couldn't be Bobby. He'd been in custody. Besides, it's hard to fire a weapon when your right wrist is badly sprained. Give him credit. He never explained how it had happened. He wanted to pay me back in kind and was waiting for his chance.

Things settled down. Deborah, shamefaced, went around recanting her "lie." She also admitted I'd caught her in bed with Bobby and thrown them both out. People were awestruck I would take such extreme action in defense of my honor. Some girls who'd previously made a point of ignoring me suddenly were very friendly and offering to console me. I would have none of it. Susan didn't come near me. She had her hands full keeping Deborah stable.

Or so Alice said one night, a week later, when she dropped by for seconds.

I laughed out loud. "What the hell?" I said. "Come in."

She did, as delicately as a Siamese cat, sniffed, looked around and said primly, "This place is a mess." She began to pick up beer and soda cans and put them in a paper grocery sack.

"What are you doing?"

"Cleaning up this dump. You guys are a public health hazard."

"Hey!" said the roommate who had declared himself a homosexual, but didn't know what to do about it. "A little respect, please."

She ignored him, hung up her coat and looked around. "This is going to take some time."

The roommate came into the living room and saw she was serious.

"Is this one of your weird sex scenes, Hamit?"

"Sure," Alice said sarcastically, "I'm going to play I'm the maid, do all the work, and then let him have his way with me, like in a cheap novel."

"Don't look a gift horse in the mouth," I said.

"I'm going out," the roommate said.

"Oh, you can both help," she said. "In fact, I insist you both do."

He paused, grinning now. "Not much of a submissive sex slave, is she?"

Alice paused. "Someone has been reading up," she said, her eyebrows arching. "Oh, my."

She continued to clean, bending over to pull newspapers off the floor.

"You guys are pigs." She loaded a stack into his arms to take downstairs, tilted her head and said, "Say that I was? I wouldn't be your slave. I'd be his. Unless he wanted to lend me to you."

Where the hell does that come from? I wondered. She'd obviously been reading up, too. And she was being a terrible tease.

"I'm a homosexual," my roommate stammered.

"Really! Are you sure? I used to think I was a dyke. Then I met him and I'm all confused. You're really sure?"

"Pretty sure," he said. There was doubt on his face.

"Stick around and find out," Alice said, moving her hips

suggestively.

He blushed. "Thanks, but I have a date."

With a guy. I knew what a big step it was and how hard it had been for him to arrange.

"Leave him alone, Alice," I said. "What's gotten into you?"

She turned and threw her arms around my neck. I got a good look at her eyes.

"You're stoned."

"Maybe." She looked over her shoulder at my roommate. "You're excused, sir."

He went to get his coat, put it on, hoisted the stack of old newspapers, and went to the door.

"I'll be back late," he said. "Good luck. I have a feeling you're going to need it."

Alice stuck her tongue out at him.

"What a brat," he laughed. He closed the door behind him and went down the stairs.

Alice said, "I didn't want to fuck him, anyway. Just you."

"You're stoned."

"So what?"

"I can't take advantage of a girl in your condition. It's not right."

"My God, you are such a fucking boy scout." She cuddled in my arms for a little and then said in that same bright, false little-girl voice: "Tell you what. Let me finish what I'm doing here and get sober, and we'll go from there." She looked up, anxious now. "Is that okay?"

"All right," I said. The place really was dirty. It needed a woman's touch.

She started to strip off her clothes, folding them carefully and putting them in the drawer that Deborah had vacated.

"What are you doing?" I thought it was a prelude to the sex I had just turned down.

"I don't want to get them dirty," she explained, as if that were the most obvious thing in the world. "You just sit there and let me work. Do some homework, Pay me no attention."

That was actually a good idea and I tried. Really I did, but she was naked. And not body-shy at all. She liked it. I made sure the door was locked, got a beer, and enjoyed the show. She did it all: vacuum, dust, clean. After an hour, the place looked better than the day we'd moved in.

She got herself a beer and plopped down next to me on the couch. With her other hand she reached down and began to play with herself.

"With you or without you, Sir. It's all the same to me."

I laughed again. "What's this 'Sir' shit about?"

She put down her beer and added her other hand between her legs. "Deb calls it 'research.' Some cheap paperbacks she found in a New York bus station. Really lurid stuff, almost comical. We read them aloud in the room at night, laughing because they are so corny. Women are always surrendering themselves to strong muscular men, and becoming sex slaves. They have to call their masters 'Sir' or they get whipped."

She threw her head back as her orgasm came. After a moment, she sighed. "I really want to be your slave, Francis. Give you complete control because it would be so easy. I could be somewhat normal and stop falling in love with other girls. Let me play at it a little, anyway."

"Why would you do that?"

"You're kind. Gentle. And you really know how to fuck. Susan's sorry she never let you have your way with her."

"Well, that's all in the past," I said.

"But we all love you," she protested. "We'll do anything for you."

I assumed it was the drugs talking.

"Too late now," I said. "One of you almost got me killed. I may have to leave town. I'm on academic probation and about to be drafted because I'm flunking half of my courses."

"Oh, no!" she said. She was genuinely distressed.

"Let's not talk about that," I said. The idea depressed me. I don't like to fail, and my father was going to be very pissed off. He paid my tuition. Wasted now.

"Am I still high?" she said.

I turned her head and looked closely at her eyes. "Yep."

She looked at her wet hands, shook her head and went into the bathroom to find a towel. Drying herself, she came back in—still naked—and sat in the chair opposite me, spreading her legs.

"No," I said, "Not yet."

She growled with frustration.

"You know, if you're serious about this sex slave stuff, you'd realize that we do it when I say, not whenever you want it."

She shook her head. "Bastard. No, you're right. I'm being bad. You should punish me."

"What makes you think I'm not?"

She laughed outright. Then she saw some of the prints from my Creative Photography class. That one I had an "A" in. She picked them up.

"These are really nice," she said.

"Thank you. Handle them by the edges, please."

She looked at a couple more. "Is this Pat?" she asked.

"Yes. Why?"

"We share a class. I like her. How'd you get her to pose?"

"Paid her. She models for the art department. And some on the side for cash. So it's a job."

"Did you fuck her, too?"

"No. I never would. It's not ethical. She's not a whore."

Alice looked up dreamily. "Maybe I should model. I don't seem to mind being naked now."

"You're high. Tomorrow you're going to remember this and be really embarrassed. You won't be able to do it straight, and if I took pictures of you right now and published them you'd be very upset with me. Besides, you're only 19. Models have to be 21, so they can sign a release."

"Oh." She put the photo of Pat back on the table.

"I like her. But she has a sad life, what with two kids and all. And her boyfriend just left her."

I wasn't really interested in Pat's problems since I had plenty of my own. In addition to the breakup, my car had been impounded for unpaid parking tickets. Fortunately, nothing of any real value was inside, since I carried my pistol all the time now. The fines were more than I'd paid for it, so I had no real reason to pay them and get it back; it was still registered to its previous owner who would be on the hook for them. As we were talking, I had been reading a textbook. Not that she wasn't nice to look at and I didn't want her. Just that she was so comfortable now that any tension between us evaporated. I'd gotten bored with her nudity.

Then Alice said something that got my full and complete attention.

"Well, she's real upset. There was no reason for it. Sonny just gets up in the middle of the night, packs all his stuff, kisses her goodbye, and leaves. It was 3 a.m. She doesn't understand it. She doesn't know what she did."

Sonny. The son-of-a-bitch the cops and I had been trying to nail for months. There was a warrant out for him, at long last, and he'd flown the coop. I remembered he'd been dating Pat, but he'd been dating a lot of other girls. It was easy for him. The drugs in his pocket made it so.

Trust Sonny to move in with the one girl who couldn't admit he was staying with her because Welfare would try to take her kids. I was sure he'd paid her. That made her an accomplice. I could give no sign of my interest in this to Alice. The drugs were out of her system now. I knew that because she'd suddenly looked down, realized she was naked, and bolted to the bedroom to get something to cover herself with as she blushed bright red.

I couldn't help it. I laughed.

She stamped her bare foot in frustration. "That's not nice!" she said, starting to tear up.

I got up and went over to her, taking her in my arms.

"It's all right. You want to go home?"

"I wasn't that stoned, damn you. I want what I came for. Sex. I want you to make love to me the way you do Deborah."

I pulled the cover away from her and looked her slowly up and down, pretending to be the hard master she'd said she wanted. She didn't flinch. She held her head high this time, a slave girl at auction.

"You'll do," I said. "What do you want to do first?"

"You know about blow jobs?"

I nodded.

"Make me do it, and do it right. Teach me."

"You've never done one?"

"I've had a cock shoved in my mouth and my head held until I choked, but I want to learn to do it slow and sensual, so I can control the man and make him beg. You ever try something like that?"

I nodded. "Deb."

"Then teach me," she demanded. So I did, since I'm such a nice guy. She was like a kid in a candy store.

CHAPTER 16

The skies changed from bright blue to a dreary metallic color. I still had to be careful. It took me a couple of days to find Pat, because nude models were assigned at random for life-drawing classes and the instructors were careful to keep gawkers from intruding. You had to be taking a class or be an art major to even get in the room. It was not something she did every day, because it was also the best-paying part-time job on campus and there was lots of competition. Not all of the models were students. One was a fifty-year old farm wife who weighed over 300 pounds. Few were men. One of those was on the Iowa football team, where the front line was reputed to play "drop the soap" in the locker room, and that was given as an excuse for their horrible losing season the previous year. He was a big showoff, that guy, and declined to use a modesty cup to cover his genitals.

My ticket in was my Creative Photography class, but even then the T.A. looked suspiciously at the 35mm Minolta around my neck.

"You can't use that in here," she objected. "The model will be exposed."

"I am trying to document the process here," I said smoothly. "By exposing the artists at work. This is a wide-angle lens. How about I stand behind her at a distance and shoot the whole room. Her face won't be shown and everyone will be in the shot."

"Yeah, but they're not naked. She'll have to agree. Pat?"

Pat came over, wearing a robe but nude underneath. Nude photos of her regularly appeared at the local art fair, done by a local photographer who was also a prime supplier of long-distance photos of the local Amish to the media, over their objections. He was no respecter of boundaries. One of those prints had ended up in the hands of a Welfare case worker as proof of her "immorality," and caused Pat lot of problems with that agency. Fortunately, it was a shot from a class and not a private session. He was too cheap to pay her on his own.

She looked at both of us, smiling at me. "Hello, Francis." The T.A., now assured that we knew each other, relaxed and told her what I wanted to do.

"It won't take long," I said. "Fifteen minutes tops, and your face won't be shown. I'll throw in a bonus for the extra work." I held up a five-dollar bill. Half a day's pay for me.

"Oh, you don't have to do that," Pat said. "We're friends, after all."

"I insist."

"Have you seen Sonny?" she asked suddenly.

I looked at her careful. It was a real question. She was anxious about him and where he might be.

"No," I said. "I've been looking for him myself."

She went back to where her school books were, took out a small pad, and then scribbled something on it. She came back over and handed the top sheet to me.

"This is where we're living now. Why don't you come see me tonight, after my kids are in bed, and pay me then?"

"I will," I said.

"And don't worry about showing my face. That ship has sailed. Everyone knows I do this, and I have nothing to be ashamed of." She walked over to the center of the room, with about thirty students waiting, slipped off her robe and began to pose for them. She was so beautiful, it took my breath away. Like a classic Greek statue.

I crept along the walls of the room, taking long shots that put her, naked, in the center, surrounded by the class working at their easels. There were interesting reactions. Some of the men turned their heads or ducked behind their drawing pads to prevent their faces being photographed. Pat was unashamed, but they were not, or at least very nervous about being seen in public with a naked woman.

I shot an entire role of Tri-X, without a flash, in about 15 minutes. I walked closer to Pat, to the annoyance of some of the students, who hissed at me to get out of the way.

"Gotta go," I whispered.

"See you tonight," she said out of the side the side of her mouth. "I'd like to have one of those."

"I'll go to the lab right now and see if I can process them."

"Great. See you tonight."

I stepped away, and she said, "And Francis?"

"Yes?"

"Bring a bottle."

I was skipping classes or showing up late for them. My class schedule was known and I worried about being shot at a second time. No target, me. The photo lab in the art building was the perfect place to hide for several hours because developing the film and making prints gave me a reason to be there. Conveniently, I still owed a final project to that instructor.

As I worked, I speculated to myself why Pat had asked me to bring a bottle. Welfare sometimes made unannounced inspections of her living quarters. "For the children's sake," they said. They thought of her as immoral, because she'd not married either father of her two boys and had the first one when she was fifteen. She was the first one in her farming family to go to college, but Welfare didn't make it easy for her. They were very intrusive, Sonny told me, and he'd been careful to stay out of view.

"So no drugs?"

"Of course not," Sonny gave me a look of disbelief. "She's not into that. I wouldn't be with her if she was. I hate fucking pot heads."

"Yet, you are reputed to be the biggest dealer in town."

"Maybe I am, and maybe I'm not," Sonny said with a smirk.

"Everyone knows this, Sonny."

"Knowing a thing and proving it are two different things," he replied. "Good luck with that." He looked hard at me then.

"I worry about Pat. She's a friend."

He leaned back a cruel smile on his face. "You can try to fuck her if you like, but all that hippie free-love stuff notwithstanding, she's still a little small-town uptight Iowa girl. One man at a time. She's not looking for love. She is looking for a husband so she can get those Welfare bitches off her back."

"You?"

"No," he admitted. "That would not be kind. I can't drag her into this."

"Into what?"

He looked irritated with himself for the slip and shook his finger at me.

"Nice try, asshole." But he was too arrogant to see me as a real threat. He just thought I was trying to get under his skin as he had, so many times, gotten under mine.

The photos of Pat modeling for that class came out very well. I was printing the best of them when my photography instructor came in and looked over my shoulder.

"Very nice composition," he said. "But you need to print the blacks deeper. Is that going to be your last class submission?"

"If you approve."

"I do, very much. You've captured a unique moment in time, demonstrated a process, and framed the whole thing beautifully. Not bad for a hack."

I'd been called a "hack" by another student in the class because he was offended by the fact that I used my camera to make money. The class, he said, should be about art, not commerce. He was baiting the instructor, who worked for several ad agencies in New York when he wasn't teaching. The instructor's reply had been scathing, inviting him to drop the class.

"Work on those blacks," the instructor said. "What are you doing these days?"

"Oh, I don't know. Hanging out, drinking, skipping class, flunking out."

"I heard something about drugs. You're not doing drugs, are you?"

He was actually concerned, I realized.

"I seem to be the only student at Iowa who is *not* doing drugs," I said. "I just broke up with my girlfriend because she won't stop."

"Sorry to hear that. You're right, It's everywhere. I was going to ban students who showed up high from my classes, but couldn't. Too many of them. I'd have to cancel the class. So I put up with their bullshit. It will get better."

"Maybe," I said, as I developed another print. He watched the image bloom in the developing fluid, waited and picked up the wet print from the fixer, turning on the white light and looking at it very carefully.

"Better," he said. "But try again."

He moved toward the door. "See you in class," he said. Perhaps he was going to say something else about what he'd heard because he murmured to himself, "Where are the police?"

The police were actually doing better now. Several dealers had been arrested and that was in the papers. If he'd heard about Deborah's false/not false accusation, he might have been wondering about me that way, but was too smart or scared to ask me outright.

That night I walked toward Pat's house along the highway out to the airport. Large stretches of the land adjacent were empty and wooded. I was wearing my black overcoat and staying well to the margin to avoid being hit from behind by some drunken frat boy. Cars zipped past me at a moderate pace, but not too often. I had a brown paper bag with a fifth of Jack Daniels in my left hand and my right on the pistol in my pocket. It was a comfort.

As I walked along the shoulder, headlights and the blare of a horn from a startled driver sometimes came from behind, warning me to stay off the road. But what came next had almost no warning—it was only the changing sound as the tires hit the gravel shoulder and a powerful engine accelerated behind me with a complete absence of headlights that made me dive for cover. I hit the ground flat after running into the woods. The ear-shattering blast of a double-barreled shotgun and buckshot shredding the trees overhead shocked me into a numb silence. Tires squealed and the assassin's vehicle sped away. I kept my head down and did not try to get a look at it. Maybe they would assume that they'd hit me. I felt perfectly sick as pain shot through my body. I lay there for several minutes, still hurting from hitting the ground hard, and wondered if they'd come back for a second try. When they didn't, I got to my feet and looked around for the whiskey and the pistol. Both were lodged in a bush about ten feet away. The whisky bottle was unbroken.

"What happened to you?" Pat asked when she opened the door. She could see how dirty I was. I walked in and she closed the door behind me. I handed her the bottle, which was unsealed and partially empty.

"Did you start without me?" she asked. She was not irritated but curious. Her wide-spaced green eyes and long nose could have made her look stern, but her lips were full, almost swollen, and her smile was kind. She reached out and touched me reassuringly. There was none of the tension generated by a "first date" back then. She smelled wonderful. The last thing I wanted to do was to turn her off, and it seemed that I'd violated one of those unspoken rules by drinking ahead rather than thinking ahead. I felt very unsure of myself.

How to explain? I certainly wasn't going to tell her about someone trying to blow my head off. She might insist I report that to the police. I didn't want it on the police blotter, which was sometimes reproduced in the Iowa City *Press-Citizen.* I already had more attention than I could use.

"Sorry," I said. "I had a couple at home since I don't have my car anymore and aren't driving. It's dark out there. I fell. Tripped on something."

She frowned. "But you're not drunk?"

"No." I could tell from her expression that drinking was okay. Falling down drunk was not. Hell of a way to start a date, I thought. Not that it was really a date. My true purpose was to find out what had happened to Sonny.

"Well, let's get you cleaned up." She took my overcoat and shook it out. Then she found a whisk broom and dusted me off. "Go in there and wash off."

I went into her bathroom, looked in the mirror and saw the dirt and the twigs in my hair and beard. I washed and combed and realized that some of the dirt wasn't coming off because it was actually a bruise. I was embarrassed.

"I'm sorry," I said. "Maybe we should do this another time."

"Nonsense," she said. "You're here and I can use some company. Sonny left me."

We went back into her living room. She curled up on the couch, tucking her feet under her and I eased myself into a chair. Involuntarily, I groaned in pain.

"Are you all right?"

"I'll live. I'm more embarrassed than anything else." She was wearing an off-the-shoulder peasant blouse and long skirt and had actually put on lipstick and make-up. She was naked underneath. So this was a date, I realized. One with no pretense. Not that I thought her "easy." And my main objective was still uppermost in my mind.

"Why did Sonny leave?" I asked. "Did you have a fight?"

"No. Everything was great between us. I thought we were happy. Then one night he wakes up at 3 a.m., gets up, packs all of his stuff, loads his car, kisses me good-bye and drives off without telling me why or where he's going. It was so odd. He was scared. I never saw him scared before."

"What about?" Like an animal in the forest, I thought. Excellent instincts. No one had tipped him about the warrant. He'd just known somehow and run away. What now?

"So you have no idea?"

"No. And I wish people would stop asking. I have enough trouble with those Welfare bitches."

I tried to be casual. "Who asked?"

"Some guy who looks like a drug dealer and hangs around the campus. Didn't give me a name. Very intense. But that doesn't make any sense. Sonny doesn't do drugs. He hates drugs. Then this cop came by. Very polite. Real old, about fifty. A detective."

"A detective?" I was alarmed.

"Very weird. Said Sonny was a friend of his and he just needed to talk to him. He was real nervous."

The leak, I thought. The policeman in Sonny's organization.

"So why are you here, Francis?" Her facial expression was ironic. She knew the conversation was probably just a prelude to the main event, but she was lonely.

"I owe you money. You asked me to come over and bring a bottle."

"Yeah. Well, I can't keep any booze in the house. It goes against me with the Welfare creeps, who keep looking for a way to take my kids and put them in foster care, 'for their own good.' No way I'm going to let that happen. I was in foster care myself. I know what goes on."

Suddenly she was blazing angry at the memory and, just as quickly, it went away. I held up the bottle and wiggled it a bit.

"I'll get some glasses," she said, bounced up and went into the kitchen. She brought back ones that had originally held jelly and had cartoon characters on the outside. She smiled ruefully.

"All I've got."

"Whatever works." I moved over to the couch and sat next to her and poured us both a healthy shot. I raised mine in a toast.

"Here's to love being a four-letter word," I said. She smiled and sipped her whiskey.

"I heard you broke up with Deborah," she said.

And suddenly I was crying! Because it hit me how much I still loved her.

Pat put down her glass and hugged me. She wasn't wearing a bra. The feel of her breasts against my face both comforted and aroused me.

"It's okay, Baby," she said softly. "I cried over Sonny, too."

I soon stopped crying, took out my handkerchief, wiped my eyes and blew my nose. We had another drink. She was really very pretty and always kind. I'd always liked her but stayed clear because of her relationship with Sonny. Despite his comments to the contrary, you didn't poach another guy's girl. There was a code.

"What happened with Deborah?" she asked.

"I caught her in my bed with another man."

"Ooooh. Not good. What did you do?"

"Thought about shooting both of them. Decided she wasn't worth prison. Threw him down the stairs. Told her to get out and not come back."

"That jealousy thing, man. It's toxic." She moved a little closer and I could feel the warmth of her body.

"You're never jealous?"

"Sometimes," she admitted. "But not with Sonny. He's actually kind of a cold fish, and not real great in the sack. We have an understanding. Most of the nights he was here, he would just read and study or work on his dissertation. He offered me money, and always has plenty of it, but I want to be my own woman. I won't be 'kept.' Put a ring on my finger or forget it."

"But you slept with him?"

"So what? I sleep with a lot of guys. I have legal troubles. My lawyer represents me *pro bono*, but we still go to a nice motel one afternoon a week. Just so he knows I'm grateful."

I nodded, absorbing that. She was far tougher than she looked. A survivor.

"I've made a lot of mistakes," she said, looking sad now, "But I learn from them."

"Tell me about foster care."

"What's to tell? It's the luck of the draw. Sometimes you get wonderful, kind people you wish really were your parents, and sometimes you get raped and beaten up." She poured herself another drink and tossed it back. The anger was back in her face.

"You were raped?"

"Twice. I don't want to talk about it and I don't want to talk about your broken heart, either. You should have seen that coming. No girl is that sexual unless she's been messed with early on."

I was momentarily stunned. I stared at her.

"I didn't know," I said after a moment. "She never said . . . "

"Why would she? It's not something you advertise."

"I wish . . . "

She cut me off. "I wish you would stop talking so much and kiss me."

So I did, and it was very different from Deborah and Alice and every other girl I'd ever had. There was no urgency and no kink. Just a sweet exploration of her body and then a very gentle entry. She took her time, but was happy and satisfied when it was over.

"Wow," she said, "Am I glad I took a chance on you! That was wonderful. You really know what you're doing. I have to sleep now. You can stay, but you have to be out by five."

"Why?"

"The Welfare bitches like to come around and check up on me, but they're lazy. They never do so outside of office hours."

She turned over, spooned her back against my chest and fell asleep almost instantly. I hugged her to me and tried to think about what she had said about Sonny. He had done the decent thing and gotten out of her life when things looked to go sour for him and his drug-running operation.

Other people were also looking for him. So what now? How did I proceed?

Everyone I'd identified as part of his operation had been at least picked up and interrogated by the detectives. Some of the "maybes" were gone or keeping their heads down. Grass had suddenly doubled in price and then doubled again. Trips to the Emergency Room for bad acid trips were not as frequent.

I never thought this was all my doing. It couldn't be. I didn't even know some of those whose names appeared on the police blotter as arrested for drug dealing, but if I'd driven Sonny out of town, then I'd done enough.

Pat was happy enough to welcome me back the following night. I brought another bottle and a large framed and matted print of her posing for that drawing class. It showed her, arms overhead like a ballet dancer, her face toward the camera, completely nude. The interesting part of it, however, was the facial expressions of the drawing students behind her. Those that could be seen ran from delight to anger, to envy, to lust—and those were just the women.

She hung it on the living room wall in plain view.

"I'm not ashamed of this," she said. "It's legal, it's a job, and I'm proud of it. I want my kids to know what their Mom will do the keep them warm, safe, and fed. Why hide that?"

I had my doubts but kept them to myself. Back then most people would have screamed "pornography" and called the cops, but that was before anyone had seen the real thing. Within five years there would be "adult" book stores all over Iowa.

Pat's major was political science, and she would graduate that spring. She had already applied to the law school and was confident of getting a scholarship that would take her off the welfare rolls for good. People had underestimated her drive because she was so sweet.

After we got that picture hung, we sat drinking and admiring it. It really was one of the best photos I made that year.

"Why do you carry that gun?" she suddenly asked. "Are you a crook?"

"No."

"Are you a cop?"

"Not exactly."

She was silent a long time. "You're after Sonny, aren't you?"

"Maybe."

She shook her head. "I never asked Sonny about his money, or how he got it, or even what his real name is. He was kind and decent and didn't judge."

Real name?! That explained a lot. He was using other names, probably complete with bank accounts and credit cards! No wonder he was so hard to find. A wild animal in the forest.

"Look," she said, "I really like you because you have all of those qualities, too, but I can tell this is not going to last. I've heard that Deborah and Susan are really kinky, and I just don't go that way, so if that's your thing, then we will stop here. I'm too damn tired for those games. They don't interest me. On the other hand, if you want to hang around and do what we did last night, then you are welcome to stay."

"Thank you," I said. "Last night was terrific. I loved every minute of it."

"Good. I do have a little kink of my own." She took my hand and led me to her bedroom where she had a number of candles burning, casting a soft warm light over everything. Against the wall, opposite the bed, was a large mirror.

"I like to watch myself." she said. "Sonny wouldn't do it. It freaked him out for some reason. Do you mind?"

Well, she was, by profession, an exhibitionist, and fearless. I looked down and saw I was rising to the occasion.

"Not at all," I said. We took off our clothes and I stood behind her, cupping her breasts in my hands. She melted in my arms, breathing deeply. In bed she liked watching me on top of her, and when I suggested that she get on top, she liked that even more.

CHAPTER 17

So we continued. I had a place to sleep nights that no one knew about. Mornings I would go to the local brokerage office where I was trading job-lot commodities options and accumulating money for my "get out of town" fund. She came in with me one time, looking around at everything. It was all new to her. The old farmers who hung out there in their faded blue overalls and green gimme caps, hedging their crops and swapping lies, were very surprised to see her with me and very nice to her.

When she left, they ribbed me a bit.

"Didn't take you long to come back from heartbreak, Hamit," said one.

"She's a student like you, you hippie freak?"

I nodded.

"Where do I know her from?" asked a third. "She looks real familiar."

"She's the girl in that naked picture you bought at the art fair that your wife made you burn." They all laughed loudly.

"Oh, yeah. I didn't recognize her with her clothes on."

I was getting pissed off. "She does that to support her kids," I said. "It's her student job at the Art Department."

They sobered and got serious. "Sorry. We didn't mean anything by it."

"You want to be careful about getting involved with a girl like that,

Hamit. Not the kind you take home to Mother."

"I would if I could," I said, "but we're going different directions. She gets her degree next summer and I'll be in the Army."

They all looked at each other.

"I'll tell you, son, I didn't think you had that in you. I thought you'd join those draft-card burners in front of the IMU. You never struck me as a soldier."

"Well, I am. My father is a Colonel in the Army Medical Corps. I grew up in the Army."

One of them stuck his hand out. "Well, good luck to you, then, and God bless."

They all shook my hand. I made my trade for the day and left, but I was gratified. They were just a bunch of old guys, but friendly enough once they saw I knew what I was doing as a trader. I was surprised that their approval meant so much to me, but it did.

I got a message from the Detective Lieutenant requesting a meeting in Cedar Rapids, thirty miles north of Iowa City. I took the bus the next morning and met him at a working man's bar near the Quaker Oats plant. They were cooking and the whole town stank of burning sugar.

He was in the booth at the very back and had a shot and a glass of water waiting for me. I drank it and sat down. He motioned for another.

"I think you've done all you can do," he said. "You're blown. People know that you are working for us. One of my junior detectives asked me about it. I denied it, but it's floating around out there, like a bad smell."

I explained how it had all happened, sparing him the details about my sex life, which would have appalled him. He took it all in, making notes in a small pocket notebook he carried.

"Well, that was bad luck," he said. "I think you're done. I think we've stopped it."

"For now."

He looked askance at me.

"In economics, we learn about supply and demand. As long as there is a demand, there will be a supply, no matter how many people you put in jail, and I am disgusted to say that more and more people are getting into it every day. It's going to be a fucking tidal wave next time. And more violent."

He nodded. "I know. How many times did they try to kill you?"

I was surprised he knew. "Two, maybe three."

"Maybe three? You're not sure?"

"The last one could have just been some drunk. A car swerved at me while I was walking out to Pat's. Almost hit me. But he was all over the road, coming and going, so I'm not sure. How'd you hear about the other two?"

"It's a small town, kid. Gunshots get reported. I put two and two together and came up with you. Why didn't you report it?"

"They missed. What could you have done about it?"

"Pulled you out for your own safety."

"Precisely. I wasn't done yet."

"Well, you are done now. Stand down. That's an order."

I won't lie. I felt an incredible rush of relief when he said that. But I maintained my cool.

He asked, "Where are you staying at night? You're never at your apartment. One of your roommates filed a missing-person report. I burned it."

"I'm with Pat, right now. Sonny's girl."

"Is that wise? He might come back, and then where will you be? Up shit creek."

"Not to worry. He left in a panic, didn't tell her where he was going, and hasn't made contact since. But here's something interesting. She said she didn't even know his real name."

The Lieutenant looked very thoughtful. "That's why we could never find him."

"Right. Do me a favor. Leave her alone. She's got enough problems."

"I don't know," he mused. "A good interrogation might jog her memory."

"She's tougher than she looks. Besides, the deal was I'd do this and you would leave my friends alone. She's friend number one right now. And I've helped her clean the house so I could find anything he left behind. Came up empty. He's a 'don't shit where you eat' kind of guy, so he probably kept the whole thing in his head and kept her out of it, out of respect."

"For her?" I could hear the sneer in his voice.

"Friends don't judge friends." I said. He let it drop.

"Okay," he nodded, "A deal's a deal. You should leave town now, you know."

"Can't do it. I have to finish the semester and ship my stuff home. I'm joining the Army. Military intelligence."

He grinned. "Well, you have the knack, I'll give you that. We'll put in a good word for you when the time comes for your security clearance."

We sat drinking for another hour, going over everything I'd seen or heard, so nothing got missed or overlooked. That night I burned my notebook.

As he was about to leave, he said, "You should at least change your appearance. We had a character around town a few years ago, big hair and beard. One day he robs the First National Bank in broad daylight. A really stupid move since everyone knows him and what he looks like.

But when we got to his house to arrest him, he was gone and his stuff was gone and his car. What was left was the hair and beard, all in the kitchen sink. Then no one could remember what he looked like without them, if we ever knew. We put out an all-points, but we never found him. He's still at large."

The Detective Lieutenant pulled out his wallet and placed a twenty-dollar bill on the table. He shook my hand.

"Goodbye, Francis. You've done a great job, but it's over. There's a good barbershop across the street. Have a shave and a haircut on me. It's the least I can do."

I picked up the twenty and put it in my shirt pocket.

"Any regrets?" he asked.

"Some, but not about this. I like to think I was on the side of the angels."

He smiled and went his way. I went to the barbershop to do as he had bid.

On the bus back to Iowa City, I wondered how much actual good I had done. I'd kept my friends safe despite their heedlessness, but none of them would ever know, much less appreciate that. I had cast myself in a negative false light and lost reputation. The demands of the undercover had stolen my time and ruined me academically, but whose fault was that? It had been my idea from the first. So, no whining and no regrets. Besides, there was a war on.

Frankie Palmer, my recruiting sergeant, was eager to get me into a part of military intelligence called the Army Security Agency. It was counter-intelligence, he assured me, or perhaps he really didn't know. Everything about ASA was Top Secret.

"But you won't have to go to Vietnam," he said, showing me a new recruiting poster with the usual Uncle Sam pointing at you portrait. "ASA Wants You" it said at the top, with "No ASA in Vietnam" below.

That month the *Daily Iowan* ran an above-the-title story about the five-year anniversary of the first American military man's death in Vietnam. James T. Davis, described as a "radioman," had been killed in a Viet Cong ambush. As I would soon learn, Davis was ASA. The recruiting poster was a lie.

The local best-selling book was *The Man Who Knew Kennedy*, written by Writers' Workshop professor Vance Bourjaily. It also explored drugs and what they were doing to society. Bourjaily, who was also a best-selling author, was a much nicer person than Nelson Algren and perhaps the best teacher of creative writing in the country. His reputation was such that I already wanted to return to Iowa after my Army service and study with him. Ultimately, I would.

My father was glad I was getting out of Iowa City, but worried that I would not be able to make it in the Army either. He assumed that I would be court-martialed and thrown out within six months. Not helpful. I was depressed enough. What was I doing with my life?

Nicholas Meyer had film reviews appearing in the *Daily Iowan* almost daily and his new play had received a rave review there. He was obviously destined for greater things, while I'd be lucky to actually stay alive long enough to be in the Army. Now that my cover was blown, my actual usefulness was over, but the opposition didn't know that and would still want to take me out. Nothing personal. Just business.

I knew that Basic Training would be hard. I began to run every day, trying to get in shape, as I began to give away or ship home my stuff. I certainly felt lighter after the barber was done with me, congratulating me on returning to "the real world" and my forthcoming Army service. Which was delayed until March 1967.

I wasn't sure that being simply shorn would be a complete disguise, so I added a couple of tricks from acting and theatre movement classes. I put a small pebble in my shoe to change my gait when walking, and went to a local thrift shop and bought a sports jacket and some dress shirts in my size. This made me look more like a T.A. from the business or engineering schools. And this worked as long as I kept my mouth shut and didn't say anything. I have a very distinctive, trained voice.

When I went back to Pat's place, she answered the door, and said, "Yes? What do you want?" in a very hostile tone.

"It's me," I said. Her mouth fell open in surprise, and then she laughed until tears came to her eyes.

"Oh, God," she said when she finally caught her breath. "I thought you were a damned Jehovah's Witness or something. Get in here!"

I walked in as she closed the door behind me, and she planted a huge kiss on me. I responded, of course. She laughed again, shaking her head.

"There's something about a man in uniform," she said. "But why this?"

"I've been told to stand down, but can't leave yet. I'm hiding in plain sight until the Army is ready for me."

"So you're going to that stock market thing in the mornings and something in the afternoon and come out here at night?"

"That okay?"

"Oh, baby. Of course it is. I want you to be safe. And I'm also really hot for you right now. You're sure not boring. How long?"

"Until March."

"I can handle that."

The next day I went to the IMU to see if I'd be recognized and walked right past Susan and Alice, who didn't even look at me or miss a step. They both looked depressed and thoughtful because my roommates couldn't tell them where I was, either.

Sleeping with Pat was almost a foretaste of marriage—easy,

comfortable, loving. I had nothing to offer her, of course, given the circumstances. We moved on after I went in the Army, with her reminding me in a letter, "I am not the girl you left behind." She knew I would volunteer for Vietnam and didn't want the heartbreak. She was convinced I would be killed there.

And she also knew that I was still obsessed with Deborah. That was the real elephant in the room that neither of us acknowledged. It would take me years to finally stop loving her and that made me a very poor marriage prospect for anyone else. Pat was very wise. She was also determined. Education was her escape from the poverty she suffered.

"They keep you down," she told me one night as we lay in each other's arms. "They make everything as hard as they can with their rules and regulations and inspections and all the rest. They try to steal your pride. Well, they can't have mine. When I become a lawyer, I'm going to fight for the people at the bottom."

In her own way, she too was a soldier. I was proud of her.

The SDS used draft-card burning as a meme to generate protests against all U.S. Government efforts to recruit students. Not only were military recruiters suddenly barred from the IMU, but a CIA recruiter's efforts were targeted by protestors, who disrupted an interview he was doing. This became front-page news. It was also a violation of the rights of any student who actually wished to volunteer for service. Who were these jerks to interfere? I was an adult. I had to go to Cedar Rapids to enlist. And this was just a foretaste of things to come. By the time I returned to Iowa City four years later, the entire country had gone over to their side and those who'd stepped up and served would be pariahs rather than heroes.

People were suggesting that I resist or run away. I couldn't even imagine that. My family was Army. I would serve whether they liked it or not. That was not patriotism. It was the call to duty. There were many other places to serve than Vietnam. Especially as a spy. I was looking forward to my new life.

I made Iowa City my home of record because I knew I would be back. It would qualify me for the much lower in-state tuition. The war couldn't last forever, I thought, and I wanted to settle there if I could. Maybe teach. Maybe open a photography studio. I was sure that my adventure as a police undercover operative would either be forgotten or forgiven by the time I returned. Certainly the cops would never say anything. They never commented on undercover operations. As long as I kept my mouth shut, I was safe, and I usually have —until now.

There's not much more to tell about this part of my life, aside from Howard Stein's reaction when I stopped by his office to tell him why I would not be in his Advanced Playwriting class that spring. He was disappointed and even more disappointed when I told him why. I could tell that he thought less of me for it.

He sighed, "It's a dirty job, but someone has to do it. Why you?"

"Why not me?" I replied.

The End

ACKNOWLEDGMENTS

Many thanks to

David McCartney,
University Archivist of The University of Iowa,
for research assistance

James Van Lydegraf,
for being a first reader

and as always to my editorial team,
Leigh Strother-Vien and Gavin Claypool.

ABOUT THE AUTHOR

Francis Hamit is a journalist, playwright, screenwriter, novelist, nonfiction author, and a 1976 graduate of the Iowa Writers' Workshop. Over his fifty-year writing career, he has held a number of other jobs to make ends meet: professional photographer, commercial-industrial real estate broker, security consultant, private detective, reporter, and sales representative. Currently, he is a film producer and historical novelist. His immediate projects include *Christopher Marlowe*, a film about the Elizabethan-era poet, playwright, and spy; and *Out of Step*, a memoir of the Vietnam War years. This book comprises the opening chapters of the latter, which continues the story of his formative years: serving in the U.S. Army Security Agency and then returning to Iowa City and the Iowa Writers' Workshop at the height of the anti-war movement.

CPSIA information can be obtained
at www.ICGtesting.com
Printed in the USA
FSOW01n0541041115
12914FS